Finding Italian Roots

Also by John Philip Colletta

They Came in Ships:
A Guide to Finding Your Immigrant Ancestor's Arrival Record

Only a Few Bones:
A True Account of the Rolling Fork Tragedy and Its Aftermath

FINDING
Italian
Roots

The Complete Guide for Americans

Second Edition

John Philip Colletta, Ph.D. 1949

First published 1993
Updated and corrected 1996
Second Edition 2003
Second printing of the Second Edition 2005
Published by Genealogical Publishing Co., Inc.
Baltimore, Maryland
Library of Congress Catalogue Card Number 2003106121
International Standard Book Number 0-8063-1741-8
Made in the United States of America

Acknowledgments

Sallyann Amdur Sack, Sharon DeBartolo Carmack, Duilio and Corinne Puett Giannitrapani, Jayare Roberts and Robert Connelly read portions of the original edition of this book in draft, and all offered helpful criticism and useful suggestions. For that kindness, I thank them.

I also thank the staff members (at that time) of the Family History Library of The Church of Jesus Christ of Latter-day Saints—Kory Meyerink, David Dilts, David Koldewyn, Diane Briggs and Terry Jeffs—for their assistance in securing many of the illustrations used in the first edition and retained in this one.

The captivating cover design by Robert Connelly and the opulent cover photograph by Jim Vecchione have received much praise since this work first appeared. I am delighted they continue to swaddle my prose. To Robert and Jim I express once again my gratitude for the gift of their respective expertise. I thank Terrence E. Barr for taking the new author's photograph.

Finally, Marcia Iannizzi Melnyk, a respected author, editor and lecturer in the field of genealogy, whose heritage is "pure Italian," graciously critiqued this revised edition in its entirety. Her thoughtful observations have improved its accuracy, and the family documents she contributed as illustrations have enhanced it visually. To Marcia I say, "*Molto grazie, cara amica!*"

For Grandma and Grandpa

Rosalia Girgenti
b. Bagheria, Sicily, 1892
d. Tonawanda, New York, 1978

&

Santo Colletta
b. Casteldaccia, Sicily, 1890
d. Kenmore, New York, 1964

The tide was colossal
They were small
Never again would they feel quite at home
Yet never did they regret it
For their family they lived
For their family seen
And yet unseen
For me

With gratitude and love

Contents

Introduction: Americans in Search of their Italian Roots

Curious to know more about your Italian ancestors? You must be. You picked up this book. You are not alone.

In Italy there is little interest in genealogy. Most Italians still live in the *paese* (community; rural neighborhood) of their ancestors.[1] Those who have moved away keep in touch easily—given modern communications and the modest size of the country—with family "back home." It requires no effort at all for Italians to retain a strong sense of their own personal heritage.

For Americans of Italian descent, however, that is not the case. Having been uprooted from the "Old World" two, three or four generations ago and replanted in the "New World," Americans must make a diligent effort if they wish to recapture their Italian heritage. And they are making that effort in ever increasing numbers.

You may be a fortunate Italian American whose strong family ties and enduring oral tradition make climbing the family tree back to the immigrant ancestor a rather quick

---

[1] Throughout this book, the first time an Italian term appears it is followed by its English equivalent in parentheses. Once introduced, however, the term will be used without translation, because the Italian terms are the ones you must master in order to use Italian records. If you come across an Italian word you do not recall from its first appearance, just check the Glossary at the back of this book for its English equivalent.

and easy task. On the other hand, your path to the past may not be so smooth. Too many years have gone by. Too many elder family members have passed on. To reach back to the generation that made the momentous transatlantic crossing, many Americans need guidance in how to find and use U.S. records.

Then, once the identity of the venerable immigrant is known, *all* Italian Americans seeking their roots face the same challenge: continuing their quest in the old records of *la patria* (the fatherland). More than ever, therefore, Americans are seeking information about genealogical resources in the United States *and* in Italy.

In 1993, responding to this demand, I prepared *Finding Italian Roots*. The first nationally published manual of its kind, it has helped thousands of Americans rediscover their personal heritage. The book was updated and corrected in 1996. But interest in tracing Italian roots grows unabated, and genealogical resources and methods continue to expand rapidly in this "Information Age." Consequently, I am delighted to present this thoroughly revised, updated and expanded edition of *Finding Italian Roots*.

The Introduction's "Glimpse of Italians in America" summarizes the phenomenal impact Italian immigration has had on the institutions and culture of the United States. Chapter 1 provides the fundamental instruction Americans need to get their quest for Italian roots off and running. Chapters 2 and 3 describe the many rich materials, published and original, that family historians should explore here in the United States before attempting to access records in Italy. This new edition pays particular attention to the electronic resources—Internet websites—now available to facilitate the search.

Chapters 4, 5 and 6 explain Italy's archival system, both civil and religious, and describe in detail Italian records of genealogical value, both historical and modern. Chapter 7 offers practical suggestions drawn from my own years of experience for getting the most out of the Italian records you find, whether in person or by mail, and for realizing the greatest success in your endeavor. It contains substantial new information necessitated by the advancement of the European Union and the expansion of electronic sources.

This edition concludes with an expanded Glossary of key Italian words and a lengthened annotated Bibliography. In sum, I have endeavored to incorporate into this new version of *Finding Italian Roots* everything necessary for it to remain "The Complete Guide for Americans" for a long time to come.

So read on, and satisfy your curiosity about your Italian forebears. Great joy lies ahead, because the more you learn about your ancestors, the more you learn about yourself!

A Glimpse of Italians in America

The first Italian immigrant to the New World was Peter Caesar Alberti. He came with the Dutch in 1635 and raised a family on Long Island. But Italian immigration was extremely meager throughout the colonial period.[2] The handful of Italians living in the United States by the early nineteenth century were mostly artisans, stonecutters, sculptors and painters from northern Italy. They tended to be political refugees or emigrants by choice rather than because of economic necessity. Many were Waldenses (see Chapter 5), and being Protestant they assimilated quickly into the dominant English Protestant culture of the cities along the Atlantic coast where their skills were in demand.

---

[2] Regarding documentation, see Bibliographic Note on page 181.

Finding Italian Roots

During the 1870s and 1880s Italians began to arrive in significant numbers. They settled for the most part in the rural, agricultural Deep South, as well as in California, where the climate resembled that of their homeland. In Louisiana, Arkansas, Mississippi and Alabama, they went into farming, operated "fancy fruits and vegetables" stands and opened restaurants. In California they planted grapevines brought from Italy, founding wineries.

Overwhelmingly Roman Catholic, these immigrants tended to establish their own communities, where they continued to practice their native customs. Indeed, the "Little Italys" of the major port cities of the East Coast (Boston, New York, Philadelphia and Baltimore), Chicago, New Orleans and smaller cities of New England and the West were beginning to form during this time period.

It was between 1890 and 1924, however, that the flow of Italians to the United States rose to unprecedented numbers and crested. Economic necessity forced *millions* of Italians to emigrate for employment. The vast majority were unschooled peasants from the overpopulated, destitute southern regions of Italy, especially Calabria and Sicily, the so-called "Mezzogiorno." From sunny fishing villages on the Mediterranean coast and remote farming communities in the interior mountains, they flocked to the factories of America's northern industrial cities; the railroad construction sites in Pennsylvania, the Midwest and West; the steel mills in Birmingham, Alabama; the canneries in southern California; the fisheries in New England; the iron range of Minnesota; and the copper and silver mines of Colorado. On steamship after steamship they came, and kept coming and coming.

At first these laborers were called "birds of passage" because they came and went seasonally, working in the United States as long as weather permitted, then returning to their families in the Old Country for the winter months.

Many came twice, three times or more, and ended their days back in their native towns. But the majority of these men eventually brought their wives and children and established their families in America. (For more information about Italian immigration, see the "General Histories of Italians in America" section of the Bibliography.)

The men, women and children of this colossal wave of newcomers have to this day remained fixed in the American consciousness as the "stereotypical Italian immigrant." They populated the "Little Italys" in cities from Providence, Rhode Island, to Miami, Florida, from Chicago to California's Napa Valley. In these crowded communities they founded their own Italian parishes, businesses and fraternal organizations. They clustered according to the dialect of their native region, Sicily or Campania, Abruzzo or Calabria.

Because these southern Italians were for the most part swarthy, having dark hair and eyes, many Americans think *all* Italians are swarthy with dark hair and eyes, which is not the case. Because they brought their southern Italian cuisines, heavy with tomato sauce, pasta and pizza, many Americans think *all* Italian cuisine consists of tomato sauce, pasta and pizza, which is not true. Because American novels, motion pictures and television series persist in portraying these Italian immigrants as gangsters and *mafiosi* (members of the Mafia), many Americans mistakenly think *all* Italian immigrants were gangsters and *mafiosi*, which is far from the truth.

Gradually, however, a more accurate and balanced picture is emerging, because today the descendants of these Italian immigrants are participating in every facet of American life and culture, from cattle ranching in Montana to trawling for shrimp off the coast of Florida, from composing operas in Santa Fe to baking pastries in Providence. In universities, corporate boardrooms, city halls, sports arenas, theaters, state legislatures and governors' mansions across the country, in the U.S. Congress, the Supreme Court and the presidential Cabinet in the White House, there are descendants of Italian immigrants.

As intermarriage among members of the diverse racial and ethnic components of American society increases, more and more Americans with surnames that do not end in a vowel are discovering that they, too, have an Italian branch in their family tree. And they are not ashamed. On the contrary, they are eager to find *more* Italian ancestors.

When Peter Caesar Alberti settled in New Amsterdam in 1635, he could not have imagined that he was just the first of millions. Now many of those millions—just like you!—are passionately engaged in rediscovering their *Italianità* (Italian-ness).

1. Starting at Home

Researching your Italian-American family begins here in the United States and progresses back into the records of Italy. Those Italian records are accessible in a number of ways: 1) searching on site in person; 2) corresponding with Italian repositories; 3) examining microfilm copies of the records; 4) using the Internet; 5) hiring a researcher in Italy; or, as is usually the case, 6) *all* of the above. However you plan to conduct your research in Italian records, it is essential that you prepare thoroughly by using the materials available here in the United States first.

Without adequate preparation you will not succeed in finding the Italian records that pertain to your family, or you may eventually find them only after spending unnecessary time, money and effort, and suffering undue aggravation. In addition, unless you leave your research in the hands of a professional genealogist, sooner or later you will have to acquire at least a minimal ability to read and write Italian. Otherwise, you will not be able to understand the informational content of your family's records once you locate them. A little high school Latin will also come in handy. The better your preparation *here*, the greater your success will be over *there*.

To get you started on your ancestral quest, therefore, this chapter and Chapters 2 and 3 provide an overview of the plentiful and multifarious resources available right here in the United States. Before you plunge into these riches, however, it is important that you know exactly what you're looking for.

Three Basic Facts You Need to Know about Your Immigrant Ancestor

To pick up the paper trail of your family on the other side of the ocean (and not someone else's family by mistake!), you will need to know three basic facts about your ancestor from Italy. As you explore U.S. sources, therefore, bear in mind that you are seeking the following:

Full Original Name. Many Italian surnames have been transformed in the United States—shortened, Americanized, spelled differently, changed completely. The reasons for this, and the stories about surname changes, are myriad. Whatever the history of your own surname may be, to pursue your genealogical research in Italian records you must first learn what your immigrant ancestor's *original* surname was. It is also important to know his or her given name or names.

Since at least the sixteenth century, both on the mainland of Italy and the islands of Sardinia and Sicily, tradition has dictated how Italian parents name their children. For this reason the same given names reappear over and over in Italian families, generation after generation. A couple's first son is given the name of the father's father; the first daughter is given the name of the father's mother. The second son is given the name of the mother's father; the second daughter is given the name of the mother's mother. Subsequent children are usually given their parents' names, or the names of favorite or unmarried or deceased aunts and uncles.

Exceptions do occur. The father's father might suggest, for example, that the grandson about to be given his name be baptized instead with the name of a son of his who died in infancy many years earlier. This is especially common when no other member of the family bears the name of that deceased infant. Such a wish would be honored, and a subsequent grandson would be named for the father's father. Or the mother's mother may ask that the granddaughter to be named for her be given instead the name of a particular saint to whom she holds a special devotion. This would be done, and a subsequent granddaughter would be named for the mother's mother.

Though the tradition cannot be assumed to have been followed with every child, knowing the birth order of siblings often provides a clue to the names of their grandparents.

Carrying this naming tradition over to America caused dilemmas for first-generation Americans, who came up with some very creative "translations" of Italian given names. If the grandmother was Crucifissa, for instance, a name whose literal translation would be Crucifix, the granddaughter might be baptized Christine. If the grandfather was Rosario (Rosary), the grandson might be called Russell. Why Vincenzo, which should be translated as Vincent, became James in the United States remains an oddity of constant wonder and speculation among Americans of Italian descent.

It is sometimes a challenge to ascertain what an ancestor's *real* given name was. Many Italians brought with them to America the custom of calling one another by nicknames rather than given names. Usually the nickname is an altered form of the given name. For instance, Pepina is short for Giuseppina, which in turn is a diminutive affectionate form of Giuseppa, meaning Josephine. If your grandmother was called Pepina, therefore, chances are good her given name was really Giuseppa. Pepina might be translated as Jo, and Giuseppina as Josie. Giovannino might be translated as Johnny, as it is the diminutive of Giovanni, meaning John, just as Antonino (Tony) is short for Antonio (Anthony). But both Giovannino *and* Antonino may be known simply as Nino.

Complicating matters is the fact that some Italians were known by a nickname that had nothing to do with their given name. My own Uncle Tony, for example, was baptized Giovanni (John). But shortly after his baptism, his father Antonio died, and his mother wanted to keep the name Antonio in the family. So she always called her son Antonio rather than Giovanni, and the name stuck. Never did Uncle Tony use his real name.

My great-great-grandfather, Ignazio Colletta, was known as *"il Mariul,"* a Sicilian pronunciation of the Italian word *mariolo*, Jew's harp. Family lore has it that he liked to play that instrument. No one ever called him anything but *"il Mariul."* Interestingly, though, *mariolo* also happens to mean rogue or knave or swindler, so Iganzio Colletta's nickname may well have contained a sly double-entendre. Stories such as these are common in Italian-American families.

It is easy to see how four or more first cousins could all bear an identical name, since all were named for the same grandparent. To be certain you are tracing *your* immigrant ancestor's roots, therefore, and not those of some collateral branch of your family tree, or those of another family altogether, two more facts must be learned.

Approximate Date of Birth. One way to distinguish among relatives bearing the same surname and given name is by age. Knowing your immigrant ancestor's approximate date of birth will enable you to distinguish him or her from numerous cousins having an identical name.

Town of Birth. Finally, genealogical research in Italian records is impossible without knowing the *comune* (town; plural is *comuni*) where your immigrant ancestor was born. This is because many civil and religious records in Italy are kept on the local level, and those that have been removed to a remote repository are still maintained according to *comune*. From the very outset, therefore, it is important to understand the fundamental administrative structure of Italy:

Italy is divided into twenty *regioni* (regions; singular is *regione*). Tuscany, Lombardy, Puglia, Sicily, Abruzzo, Campania are all *regioni*. Each *regione* contains from one to nine *provincie* (provinces; singular is *provincia*). The five *provincie* of Campania are Avellino, Benevento, Caserta, Naples and Salerno. Each *provincia* contains many *comuni*, one of which serves as the *capo luogo* (provincial capital). The name of the province and the name of its *capo luogo* are always the same. The *capo luogo* of the province of Trapani is the city of Trapani; the *capo luogo* of the province of Pavia is the city of Pavia. Some Italian communities are so small they do not have their own mayor, but rather fall within the administrative jurisdiction of a nearby *comune*. These are called *frazioni di comune*, or simply *frazioni* (villages; singular is *frazione*).

As Chapter 4 will elaborate, Italy as a unified nation is young. Its borders, not established until 1870, have been redrawn as late as 1918. The country encompasses remarkably diverse traditions and dialects. Until recent times, therefore, Italians have identified more strongly with their own *paese* than with *Italia*. Rather than calling themselves *Italiani*, immigrants at the turn of the twentieth century called themselves *Siciliani* or *Abruzzesi*, for example, or *Calabresi*, after the *regione* they came from, or perhaps *Palermitani*, *Napolitani* or *Genovesi* after their *provincia*. Since the *capo luogo* of every province has the same name as the province, this can be misleading. My grandfather, Santo Colletta, always said he was from "Palermo," *not* because he was a native of that *city*, but rather because he hailed from one of the many villages within that *province*.

Therefore, as you seek out and examine historical resources pertaining to your family here in the United States, be particularly vigilant to learn these three basic facts about your immigrant ancestor: 1) full original name; 2) approximate date of birth; and 3) *comune* of birth.

Where to Find These Three Basic Facts . . . and Much More

There are many ways to discover the three basic facts about your immigrant ancestor. Rarely, however, will you find the facts all together in a single source. Rather, you will have to gather them together, or deduce them, by combining information gleaned from several sources. Below is an overview of sources you will want to explore thoroughly. As you peruse them, you will learn much more about your immigrant ancestor than simply his or her full original name, approximate date of birth and town of birth. You will glean a wealth of fascinating details about your Italian ancestor's day-to-day life in the United States. And the more information you have, the more productive and successful your work in Italian records will be.

Interviewing Relatives. Stories passed on orally from generation to generation form the bedrock of family history. Your first step toward rediscovering Italian ancestors who lived long ago, therefore, is to harvest the memories of relatives who are still living today. Since most Americans of Italian descent are removed just two, three or four generations from their immigrant ancestors, interviewing relatives tends to be especially rewarding for them.

Older relatives who knew your immigrant ancestor or the first generation of your family in America, are likely to have heard stories about the immigration experience: who came when, from where, and how and why. They may have heard anecdotes about the family's native village in Italy.

Learn as much as you can about the place of origin, for many Italian *comuni* have the same or similar name: what *regione* of Italy is it in, and what *provincia*; what is the nearest major city, and how far away is it; how many churches are there in the village, and what are they called; is there a synagogue, a railroad station; is the town in the hills or on the shore? . . . Such details may mean the difference between success and failure in distinguishing the *comune* you want from others of the same name.

Elderly relatives often know the name of the steamship that brought your immigrant ancestor to America, and they may have been told stories about how the family's surname changed, and why. There is no way of knowing what fascinating and useful information your relatives' memories hold until you start asking questions.

Interviewing relatives not only gives you the foundation upon which all of your future research will be based, but provides personal information about your ancestors as real people too. Learning an ancestor's nickname or occupation, for example, or which feast days the family celebrated and with what special foods, or the dialect the family spoke, is more than just fascinating biographical detail. Such information also supplies clues regarding the path your research should take in Italian records. It might lead you to explore resources you would not otherwise have thought of searching.

Family lore is rarely correct in every detail. With generations of retelling, the old stories become elaborated, distorted, confused. Nevertheless, most family tales contain a kernel of truth. Besides, regardless of its verifiable accuracy, oral tradition gives members of a family a sense of place in the world, a sense of belonging, a sense of who they are. Since Italian Americans generally relish reminiscing about their family's past, you may find that the first step in discovering your roots—talking with relatives—turns out to be the most enjoyable and memorable step.

Effective interviewing, however, is not magic. There are techniques to be employed and etiquette to be observed. Guidelines for conducting productive interviews are explained in genealogical manuals and books about recording oral history (see Bibliography). Sharon DeBartolo Carmack's *Italian-American Family History: A Guide to Researching and Writing About Your Heritage* is a particularly fine primer on the subject.

Materials at Home. An integral part of interviewing relatives is exploiting family keepsakes and heirlooms. Contacting aunts, uncles and cousins usually results in the discovery of old family photographs, passports, letters, military discharge papers, citizenship certificates, remembrance cards from funerals, steamship ticket stubs, postcards depicting the ancestral *comune* and other treasured mementos. All of these are valuable sources of information (see illustrations on pp. 27–29). Photo albums and scrapbooks are especially effective for sparking memories and eliciting conversation about the ancestors.

Similar to family lore, keepsakes found in relatives' homes often reveal more about your ancestors than just the bare facts of their immigration story. Insight into an ancestor's temperament or motives may show up in the most unexpected places.

My grandmother Rosalia Colletta, for example, kept an old tattered passbook from the *Casse di Risparmio Postale* (Postal Savings Bank) of Rome. The stamped numbers in it, showing that my grandparents sent modest monthly deposits overseas until late 1929, reveal that they originally intended to return to Italy. But the Depression intervened and ultimately caused them to remain in America. Moreover, the fact that my grandmother did not discard the

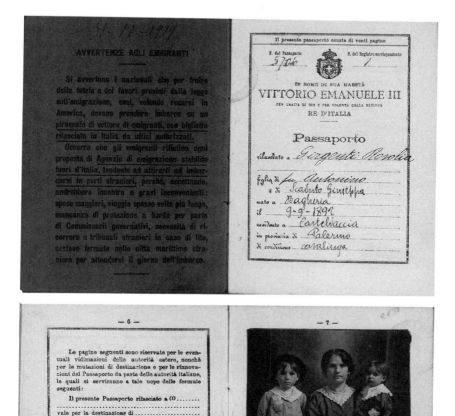

Portion of passport belonging to Rosalia Girgenti and her son and daughter, Ignazio and Rosalia Colletta. Note that the mother appears under her maiden name, while the children are under their father's surname. Interior pages provide additional information about the family. (*From the author's collection.*)

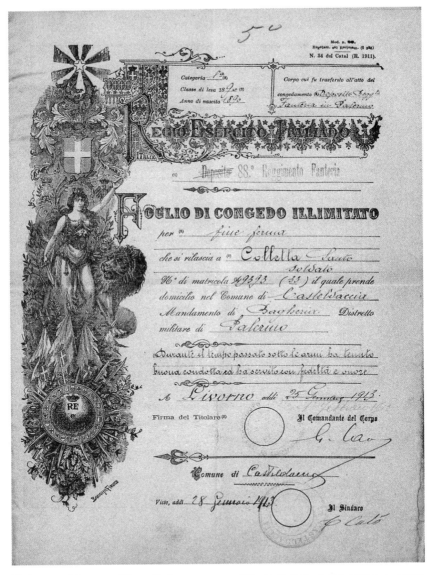

First page of 4-page military discharge papers of Santo Colletta dated 1 February 1913. Interior pages contain a wealth of information about the soldier and his family. (*From the author's collection.*)

Steamship ticket stub showing receipt of payment for three 3rd class places on the SS *Patria,* leaving Palermo on 1 February 1920. Note that the mother is listed under her maiden name and pays full fare; child's place costs one-half fare, baby's place costs one-quarter. Reverse of stub informs passengers of meals to be provided on board and suggests additional provisions to bring. (*From the author's collection.*)

passbook when Benito Mussolini nationalized these immigrant accounts in 1938, but kept it her entire life, also says something about my ancestors. It appears they never gave up hope that one day their hard-earned savings would be returned to them.

On the other hand, your own immigrant ancestor's story may be quite the contrary. A citizenship certificate dated within four years of his arrival shows not only that the immigrant was eager to stay for good, but also that he intended to participate actively in American public life.

Artifacts such as a great-grandmother's hand-embroidered linens or the crude wooden foot locker that a great-grandfather toted throughout his military service in the Italo-Turkish War may yield no genealogical data. But such family treasures do supply precious insight into the ancestor's experiences, skills or interests. When examining keepsakes and heirlooms saved by relatives, therefore, be alert and overlook no clue to a better understanding of the distinct individuals your Italian ancestors were.

Many families have at least one relative—a spinster great-aunt, an aged uncle—who is known to have amassed such mementos over the years. As you conduct your interviews, be sure to ask who in the family has any precious documents or artifacts. Then contact those relatives and examine the treasures while their location is still known.

Organizing Your Information

The amount of information you accumulate will increase rapidly; organizing it from the start is essential. Pedigree charts and family group sheets serve this purpose.

Pedigree charts (see illustration on p. 31) keep track of who's who in your family tree. They display the names of your direct ancestors together with essential personal data: birth date and place; marriage date and place; death date and place. Family group sheets (see illustration on pp.

Pedigree Chart

Chart no. _____
No. 1 on this chart is the same
as no. _____ on chart no. _____

8 Giovanni IANNIZZI
B: abt 1779   cont. ___
P: Grotteria, Calabria, Italy
M: bef 1807
P: Grotteria, Calabria, Italy
D: 1 MAY 1857
P: Grotteria, Calabria, Italy [CR#34]

4 Francesco IANNIZZI
B: 1 NOV 1810
P: Grotteria, Calabria, Italy [CR#128]
M: 28 JAN 1842
P: Grotteria, Calabria, Italy [CR#2]
D: bet 1872 and 1875
P:

9 Caterina ANGILLETTA
B: abt 1780   cont. ___
P: Grotteria Calabria, Italy
D: 11 SEP 1860
P: Grotteria, Calabria, Italy [CR#98]

2 Giovanni Giuseppe IANNIZZI
B: 17 NOV 1842
P: Grotteria, Calabria, Italy [CR#142]
M: 1 NOV 1860
P: Grotteria, Calabria, Italy [CR#19]
D: aft 11 NOV 1909
P: Italy

10 Antonino MESITI
B: abt 1773   cont. ___
P: Grotteria, Calabria, Italy
M:
P:
D: 30 JAN 1843
P: Grotteria, Calabria, Italy [CR#10@70y]

5 Francesca MESITI
B: 29 NOV 1810
P: Mammola, Calabria, Italy [CR#218]
D: bet 1860 & 1909
P:

11 Elizabetta FERRARO
B: abt 1788   cont. ___
P: Grotteria Calabria, Italy
D: 5 JAN 1839
P: Grotteria, Calabria, Italy [CR#2]

1 Cosimo Bruno IANNIZZI
B: 19 DEC 1875
P: Grotteria, Calabria, Italy [CR#204]
M: 11 JUN 1911
P: Boston, Suffolk, MA/Saugus, Essex, MA
D: 1 JAN 1966
P: S. Paris, Oxford, ME

12 Bruno ZAVAGLIA
B: abt 1756   cont. ___
P: Mammola, Calabria, Italy
M:
P:
D: 30 AUG 1841
P: Grotteria, Calabria. Italy [CR#84]

Amelia BRUNO
Spouse

6 Domenico Antonio ZAVAGLIA
B: abt 1798
P: Grotteria, Calabria, Italy
M: 4 MAY 1825
P: Grotteria, Calabria, Italy [CR#11]
D: 11 DEC 1868
P: Mammola, Calabria, Italy [CR#259]

13 Francesca ZAVAGLIA
B: abt 1772   cont. ___
P: Mammola, Calabria, Italy
D: 13 OCT 1852
P: Grotteria, Calabria, Italy [CR#92]

3 Maria ZAVAGLIA
B: 27 DEC 1837
P: Grotteria, Calabria, Italy [CR#92]
D: 20 SEP 1898
P: Grotteria, Calabria, Italy

14 Domenico AGOSTINO Apone
B: abt 1787   cont. ___
P: 28y in 1815
M: bef 1811
P:
D: 14 MAY 1851
P: Mammola, Calabria, Italy [CR#47]

7 Angiola\Angela AGOSTINO
B: 5 FEB 1813
P: Grotteria, Calabria, Italy
D: 26 OCT 1870
P: Mammola, Calabria, Italy [CR#246]

15 Anna SCALI
B: abt 1793   cont. ___
P: Grotteria, Calabria, Italy
D: 16 AUG 1857
P: Grotteria, Calabria, Italy [CR#59]

Pedigree chart of Cosimo Bruno Iannizzi showing his parents, grandparents and great-parents. Notice the standard numbering system for keeping track of direct ancestors: the father's number is always twice the child's, and the mother's number is always twice the child's plus one. (The "CR" numbers in brackets refer to the place on the Family History Library microfilm for the *comune* where that particular "Civil Record" appears.) Any branch of the family may be extended by appending another chart; for example, a chart beginning with #13, Francesca Zavaglia, will show her father as #26, her mother as #27 and so forth. (*Courtesy of Marcia Iannizzi Melnyk.*)

Family Group Sheet

4 MAR 2003

Husband	Francesco IANNIZZI	
Birth	1 NOV 1810	Grotteria, Calabria, Italy [CR#128][1]
Misc	27 APR 1860	witness to a document; Grotteria Calabria, Italy [CR#35 death][2]
Death	bet 1872-1875	
Burial		
Marriage	28 JAN 1842	San Nicola di Franco, Grotteria, Calabria, Italy [CR#2][3,4]
Father	Giovanni IANNIZZI (b abt 1779)	
Mother	Caterina ANGILLETTA (b abt 1780)	

Wife	Francesca MESITI	
Birth	29 NOV 1810	Mammola, Calabria, Italy [CR#218][5]
Birth	abt 1811	Grotteria, Calabria, Italy
Death	bet 1860 & 19	
Burial		
Father	Antonino MESITI (b abt 1773)	
Mother	Elizabetta FERRARO (b abt 1788)	
Other spouse	Giuseppe FRANCONARI	
Marriage	8 NOV 1830	S. Nicola di Franco, Grotteria Calabria, Italy [CR#32][6]

Children

1 M	Giovanni Giuseppe IANNIZZI	
Birth	17 NOV 1842	Grotteria, Calabria, Italy [CR#142][7]
Baptism	20 NOV 1842	Chiesa San Nicola di Franco, Grotteria, CAL, Italy[8]
Misc	21 OCT 1891	witness to death record; Grotteria, Calabria, Italy [CR#97][9]
Misc	OCT 1897	witness to death record; Grotteria, Calabria, Italy [CR#113][10]
Death	aft 11 NOV 1909	Italy
Burial		
Spouse	Maria ZAVAGLIA	
Marriage	1 NOV 1860	S. Nicola di Franco, Grotteria, Calabria, Italy [CR#19][11]
Spouse	Angiola SCALI	
Marriage	aft 28 NOV 1901	
Spouse	Maria Filomena LAURO	
Marriage	11 NOV 1909	Grotteria Calabria, Italy [CR#31][12]

2 F	Rosa Maria IANNIZZI	
Birth	6 DEC 1845	Grotteria, Calabria, Italy [CR#168 or 169][13]
Death	29 JAN 1846	Grotteria, Calabria, Italy [CR#8][14]
Burial		
Marriage		

Prepared 4 MAR 2003 by: Marcia Iannizzi Melnyk	Comments:

FAMILY NOTES

Marriage: Grotteria 1842 marriages #2; license recorded 27 Jan 1842 to Francesco IANNIZZI of Grotteria, 31 yrs, born in Grotteria, bracciale, figlio di Giovanni IANNIZZI, bracciale of Grotteria and Caterina ANGILLETTA of Grotteria TO Francesca MESITI of Grotteria, 31 yrs, born in Mammola, resides in Grotteria, figlia di Antonino MESITI, bovaro, of Grotteria and Elisabetta (fu) FERRARO. side margin notes that marriage took place on 28 Feb 1842 at the parish of San Nicola di Franco

HUSBAND NOTES: Francesco IANNIZZI

Birth: Grotteria births 1810 #128; recorded on 2 Nov 1810 at Grotteria; Giovanni IANNIZZI, bracciale, in 29th year of age testified to the birth of his son Francesco IANNIZZI at 1900 hours on 1 Nov 1810 to his wife, Caterina ANGILLETTA, aged 31, resides in region of San Nicola di Franco; witnesses are Vincenzo BARRILARO, aged 46, bracciale & Nicodemo PAPALUCA, aged 62, bracciale

Misc: Grotteria 1860 deaths #35 (folio #18): LUCA, Giuseppe died 26 Apr 1860 at 63 yrs of age; widower of Anna MESITI; witness was IANNIZZI, Francesco [fu Giovanni], 50y, bracciale of Grotteria

Family group sheet of the Iannizzi family: Francesco, his wife, Francesca Mesiti, and their two children, Giovanni and Rosa Maria. The form records all the information gathered so far on this particular family, with notations showing precisely where each piece of biographical data was found. (*Courtesy of Marcia Iannizzi Melnyk.*)

Family Group Sheet

WIFE NOTES: Francesca MESITI

Birth: Mammola births 1810 #218; recorded on 29 Nov 1810 at 1600 hours; Antonio MESITI, bracciale, age 40, of Mammola testified to the birth of his daughter Francesca MESITI at 7 o'clock on 29 Nov 1810 to his wife, Elizabetta FERRARO

CHILD NOTES: Giovanni Giuseppe IANNIZZI

Birth: Grotteria births 1842; ordinance #142; dated 18 Nov 1842 at 1500 hours; Francesco IANNIZZI (di Giovanni), 32 yrs old, bracciale, resides in Grotteria (rione Nucara) testifies to the birth of a male child to be named Giovanni; mother is his wife Francesca MESITI (di Antonio), 30 yrs old, contadina; witnesses are Bruno ARCURI (fu Vincenzo), 46 yrs old, bracciale, of Grotteria & Domenico FRANCONARI Picarella, 56 yrs old, bracciale, of Grotteria; baptism took place on 19 Nov 1842 at Chiesa San Nicola di Franco.

Misc: Giuseppe IANNIZZI (fu Francesco), age 51y, bracciale of Grotteria witnessed the death record for a Maria ZAVAGLIA, 29y who died at 1 pm on 21 Oct 1891 in Grotteria. She was the daughter of fu [Guinoro ?] ZAVAGLIA and di Caterina ZAVAGLIA of Grotteria; she was single and died at contrada Nucara: witnesses were Vincenzo BELCASTRO (di Benedetto), 25y, vaticale and Vincenzo FERRARO (di Ilario), 29y, contadino, both of Grotteria

Misc: Grotteria 18987 deaths #113; SALERNO, Immaculata died Oct 1897 @ 1 yr and 3 mos of age; d/o Carmelo & Immaculata CARABETTA; witness to document was IANNIZZI, Giuseppe, fu Francesco

CHILD NOTES: Rosa Maria IANNIZZI

Birth: Grotteria 845 birth index lists Rosamaria IANNIZZI as being born 6 Dec 1845; daughter of Francesco & Francesca MESITI but the record is not on the film. Number 168 & 169 are missing from the records.

Death: 1846 Grotteria deaths #8: IANNIZZI Rosa Maria d 29 Jan 1846 @ 3 months of age; daughter of [di] Francesco IANNIZZI & [di] Francesca MESITI

SOURCES

1. Reggio Calabria Civil Records. LDS film #1518218.
2. Ibid. Grotteria 1860 #35.
3. Stato Civile Records. Grotteria 1842; #2.
4. Reggio Calabria Civil Records. LDS film#160471.
5. Stato Civile Records. Mammola 1810 #218.
6. Reggio Calabria Civil Records. LDS film #1604071.
7. Ibid. LDS film #151821.
8. Stato Civile Records. Grotteria 1842; ordinance #142.
9. Reggio Calabria Civil Records. 1891 Grotteria #97.
10. Ibid. Grotteria 1897 #113.
11. Stato Civile Records. Grotteria 1860 #19.
12. Reggio Calabria Civil Records. Grotteria 1909 #31.
13. Ibid. LDS film #151821.
14. Ibid. LDS film #1547406.

32–33) provide an organized format for recording additional information about your direct ancestors, as well as facts about their brothers and sisters. These are easily expanded by appending as many pages as you need. Also—very important!—they provide a place for you to record the sources where you obtained each piece of information.

Traditionally, pedigree charts and family group sheets have been gathered into a three-ring binder, while additional materials, such as photocopied documents and audiotapes of interviews, have been stored in manila folders labeled clearly with appropriate surnames. Blank pedigree charts and family group sheets are easily obtainable from genealogical bookstores, they may be downloaded from various Internet websites—**www.familysearch.org**, to mention but one—or you may fashion your own. In addition, they are generated by genealogy software.

Genealogy software programs abound, and you may well decide that this is the easiest way to keep track of the mountains of information you are collecting. These programs not only store all of your data, but also generate charts and family group sheets at your command. What is more, using a scanner you may incorporate precious family photographs into your archive, and some of these programs also provide the option for you to write and print out an extended family narrative. Family Tree Maker, The Master Genealogist, Personal Ancestral File, Generations, Family Reunion—these are just a few examples of genealogy software programs; there are others. Each offers slightly different features. To help you decide which software product suits your needs best, genealogy magazines and the newsletters and journals of genealogical societies (discussed below) publish articles comparing and rating products regularly.

Whether you choose to stick to traditional methods or master twenty-first-century software, from the very outset of your genealogical investigation it is imperative that you organize what you learn, as you learn it, in a systematic way, noting your sources.

Joining a Genealogical Society

It is both helpful and great fun to belong to a genealogical society. Three major organizations help their members research their Italian heritage.

The oldest, founded in 1987 and headquartered in Las Vegas, is POINT (**P**ursuing **O**ur **I**talian **N**ames **T**ogether). Its journal, *POINTers*, is the only American quarterly published nationally that is devoted exclusively to Italian genealogical research. It serves as an informal vehicle for members to exchange information about their experiences with resources and methodologies, both here and in Italy, a kind of informal clearinghouse of general information about Italian-American family research. The *POINTers* databank of Italian surnames being researched by members, and the biennial seminars POINT sponsors, provide excellent venues for networking with other researchers facing the same challenges you face. A distant cousin of yours on the other side of the country may already be working on a branch or two of your family tree. Visit POINT's website at **http://www.point-pointers.net**.

The Italian Genealogical Group headquartered in Bethpage, New York, has been helping Italian Americans of the greater New York City metropolitan area find their ancestors for many years. Its newsletter, published ten times a year, is full of useful information and instruction. The organization sponsors an annual seminar, and its members are busy up-loading large and useful databases to its website, **www.italiangen.org/default.stm**. You cannot do Italian genealogy without visiting it!

To cite but four of the valuable databases now available at the Italian Genealogical Group's website, there are name indexes to naturalizations made in: (1) Nassau County, 1899–1986; (2) Suffolk County, 1853–1990; (3) Military Camps, New York, 36,000 servicemen from all over the United States; and (4) Southern District of New York (Manhattan and Bronx), 1906–1949. (For further information about U.S. naturalization records, see pages 72–77.)

The Italian Genealogical Society of America, based in Peabody, Massachusetts, is most active in New England. Its activities—publishing a quarterly newsletter, holding quarterly meetings with guest speakers and co-sponsoring conferences with larger genealogical societies—are intended not only to assist members in their pursuit of ancestors, but also to help members share and celebrate together in a personal way their "Italian-American experience." Visit IGSA's website at **www.Italianroots.org.**

Given the broad-based genealogical activity among Americans of Italian descent today, taking full advantage of these societies and their publications, seminars and websites will prove invaluable in your quest for your roots.

2. Published Resources

Having interviewed relatives, examined family documents and heirlooms, and joined a genealogical society, you now have sufficient information on your charts and group sheets to begin exploring published materials found in libraries and on the Internet. Books and journal articles pertaining to Italian-American history and genealogy have been multiplying rapidly over the past three decades.

Before the American Bicentennial and the publication of Alex Haley's *Roots*, before the popularity of ethnic cooking and summertime ethnic festivals in American cities, before scholars undertook their reexamination of immigration history and their reevaluation of the "melting pot" theory, genealogy in the United States was primarily the domain of the "blue bloods." Descendants of the *Mayflower* passengers, Daughters of the American Revolution and heirs to the illustrious first families of Virginia researched their family trees.

Over the past thirty years, however, that has changed dramatically. Now Americans of every hue and heritage are engaged in tracing their roots, and this rise in ethnic interest, pride and identification has engendered increased scholarly activity and a boom in popular and university publishing.

The Bibliography at the end of this manual lists books and articles that are now available in bookstores and libraries to help you research your Italian ancestry. But the listing is selective, not comprehensive. New works appear every year. As the Introduction has shown, the Italian-American experience is as broad and as varied as the continent between the Atlantic and Pacific.

Here is a sampling of the different kinds of published resources you will want to look for, depending on who your Italian ancestors were, where they settled and how they participated in the life of their community. For complete author and publisher information, consult the Bibliography. For many more works like these, visit your local public library.

Italians in the United States

A variety of readily accessible works contain an enormous amount of detailed information about individual Italian immigrants, their families and their descendants.

Collective Biographies of Italian Americans. Collective biographies such as Carlevale's *Who's Who among Americans of Italian Descent in Connecticut* or the *Directory of Italian-Americans in Commerce and Professions* contain thousands of biographical sketches of Italian Americans living in the United States at the time of publication. You might find your immigrant ancestor discussed in such a work.

Even if you do not, though, you may still come across other, unfamiliar individuals with your family name. Noting where they came from in Italy may help localize the geographic area where your own people lived, and that knowledge will help establish the geographic parameters of your future research in Italian records.

In addition, taking note of surnames that differ from your own by only one or two letters may also be useful, since one or more of these may turn out to be historical "variants" of your own name. Throughout your research remain alert to all possible variant spellings of your surname, just to be sure you do not overlook any lead to further information.

Histories of Italian Communities in the United States. Detailed accounts of the historical development of Italian communities all over the country are becoming ever more numerous. Such histories exist for specific cities, as in the case of Schiavo's *The Italians in Chicago: A Study of Americanization;* Mormino's *Immigrants on the Hill: Italian Americans in St. Louis, 1882–1982;* and Juliani's *Building Little Italy: Philadelphia's Italians Before Mass Migration.* They exist for many states; Starr's *The Italians of New Jersey: A Historical Introduction and Bibliography* is an example. And they exist for specific geographic regions—Casso's *Staying in Step: A Continuing Italian Renaissance (A Saga of American-Italians in Southeast United States)* and the Library of Congress exhibition catalog, *Italians in the Northwest,* are examples of such histories.

If you find a history of the community where your family settled, it may contain information about your own immigrant ancestors. Even when it does not, though, it still provides valuable historical background which will help you better understand the life they lived.

To locate collective biographies of Italian Americans and histories of Italian communities in the United States, conscientious searching in libraries with substantial collections may be required. University libraries tend to be rich in these types of book, since many of them grow out of doctoral dissertations. Research centers that house Italian-American collections (see "Private Repositories with Italian Collections," p. 58) are also likely to have such books. Since the catalogs of most libraries and research centers are now searchable on the Internet, finding such works is easier than ever.

Published Genealogies. Given the heightened interest in genealogy among Italian Americans today, you can never be sure that a distant cousin of yours whom you may not have seen in years, or whom you may just have met recently, has not already published something about your family. One recent and excellent example of an Italian-American family history is Sharon DeBartolo Carmack's *The Ebetino and Vallarelli Family History: Italian Immigrants to Westchester County, New York, in the Early 1900s, Including Descendants to 1990* (Anundsen Publishing Co., 1990). Though genealogical publishing is still young among Italian Americans, more such histories will surely be appearing in coming years.

Search the catalogs of the Library of Congress in Washington, D.C. (**www.loc.gov**), Family History Library in Salt Lake City, Utah (**www.familysearch.org**), and Allen County Public Library in Fort Wayne, Indiana (**www.acpl.lib.in.us**)—three major genealogical collections—to learn whether a family history of a surname you are working on has been published. Search also the catalogs of the public library and historical society in the community where your ancestors lived.

City Directories. Scores of Italian immigrants and their children resided in urban centers and were listed in city directories. These directories, which were normally published annually, list in alphabetical order the city's male residents with their home addresses, occupations and, sometimes, places of employment. By the turn of the twentieth century, when Italians were immigrating *en masse*, single working women were also listed, and wives who did not work outside the home were sometimes named in parentheses after their husband's name (see illustration on p. 41).

City directories also provide information about the municipal government, police and fire departments, churches,

VAL. REIS PIANO CO. E. J. PIPER GENERAL MANAGER 1005 OLIVE ST.

| 150 | BAR | GOULD'S 1908 DIRECTORY | BAR |

CAPITAL $1,700,000   Surplus and Undivided Profits **$1,700,000**

THE MERCHANTS-LACLEDE NATIONAL BANK OF ST. LOUIS

UNITED STATES DEPOSITORY.

BARSANTI & PIEROTTI (Samuel Barsanti and Peter Pierotti), Proprs. The Lindell Fruit Store, 309 N. Grand av. Tel. Bell Lindell 2365
Barsell Louis shoe r 2900A Lucas av
Barselotti Allesio lab r 2352 Carr
Barselotti Francesco lab r 2352 Carr
Barselotti Pasquale statues 2352 Carr
Barselotti Pellegrino lab r 2352 Carr
Barsha John car r 8021 N Bway
Barshall John janitor r 836 S 8th
Barski David tailor r 1726 Biddle
Barsloue Joseph L team r 1316 Arsenal
Barsmeyer John insp r 1205 Wright
Barsotti Angelo O helper r 3007 N Newstead av
Barstel Henry paint r 5118 Bulwer av
Barstow Charles W agt American T & T Co r Kirkwood
Barstow Daniel G sec Davenport Combination Filter & Cooler Co 220 Market r Glendale
Barstow Theodore G pres Davenport Combination Filter & Cooler Co 220 Market r Glendale
Bart Annie dressmkr 4273 West Belle pl
Bart Frank lab r 2804 Benton
Bart Joseph clk r 2804 Benton
Bart Michael millwkr r 2811 Salena
Barta Annie wid Vincent r 1728 S 11th
Barta Bernard molder r 4718 Nebraska av
Barta Emanuel molder r rear 1806 S 13th
Barta Vincent molder r 1312 Allen av
Bartance William B clk r 1511 Market
Barteau Edward car r 8540 N Bway
Barteau James H rope r 5639 Maffitt av
Barteau Julius foreman r 8540 N Bway
Barteau Victor helper r 8540 N Bway
Bartee George lab r 1913 Morgan
Bartee Thomas barber r 2629 Pine
Barteiger Alexander cabmkr r rear 1908 Sullivan av
Barteiger Elizabeth C wid Alexander F r rear 1908 Sullivan av
Bartel Albert blksmith r rear 1903 Blair av
Bartel Ferdinand dentist 3553 Park av r Belleville
Bartel Frederick J dentist 506 N Vandeventer av r 3883 Washington boul
Bartel Henry cond r 2701A Osage
Bartel Henry cutter r 2703A Shenandoah av
Bartel Lawrence woodwkr r 2017 Destrehan
Bartel Louis W dentist 2603 Cass av
Bartel Michael watch r rear 1903 Blair av
Bartel New York Bird Store 523 Franklin av
Bartel Nicholas lab r 3109A Alfred av
Bartel Otto blksmith r 2713 N Bway
Bartel Otto woodwkr r 2017 Destrehan
Bartel Sebastian lab r 3109A Alfred av
Bartel William chair r 2017 Destrehan
Bartel William clk Ry Mail Service r 3422 California av
Bartel William tin r 407 Duchouquette
Bartelheimer Frederick cigar r 2514A University
Bartell George E barber 6118 Minerva av r 1269 Hodiamont av
Bartell William foreman r 1518 Franklin av
Bartello Peter bartdr r 14 N Levee
Bartelme August F wagon r 4118 N King's Highway boul
Bartelme Emil shoe r 4118 N King's Highway boul

Bartels Herman Rev St John's German Evan Luth Church r 3736 Morgan Ford rd
Bartels John carp bds 933 Wyoming
Bartels John lab r 400 S 2d
Bartels John lab r 4834 Bircher
Bartels John B driver r 2829 N 19th
Bartels John H (Bartels Copper & Sheet Iron Works) 1601 N 14th
Bartels John L whitener r 3728 N 21st
Bartels L W physician City Hospital
Bartels Martin C contr 3738 Morgan Ford rd
Bartels Minnie S wid William r 3910 Parnell
Bartels Otto C clk Wabash R R r 3738 Morgan Ford rd
Bartels Otto F iron r 1450 Mullanphy
Bartels Peter C butcher r 3728 N 21st
Bartels Richard L driver r 3821 Garfield av
Bartels Theodore B clk Wabash R R r 3738 Morgan Ford rd
Bartels Theresa r 2123 Bismarck
Bartels Werner tin r 1908A Hebert
Bartels William finisher r 1501 Destrehan
Bartels William lab r 4021 Pennsylvania av
Bartels William paint 4328 Blair av
Bartels William C printer r 3007A Indiana av
Bartels William J bricklyr r 3910 Parnell
Bartels William P chemist r 1908A Hebert
Bartels William S music r 1501 Destrehan
Bartenders Protective & Benevolent League, 918 Pine
Bartenings Joseph lab r rear 1453 S 2d
Bartens Alexander J dept mngr Shallcross P & S Co r 2738 Russell av
Bartens Bertha A steno Kinloch Paint Co r 2738 Russell av
Bartens Henry F physician 2738 Russell av
Bartens Otto C cashier Shallcross P & S Co r 2738 Russell
Barter Angus J student r 4033 Botanical av
Barter Charles motor r 2431 Fall av
Barter Edmund bkpr r 1416A Union boul
Barter Fannie C teacher r 1435 N Grand av
Barter Honora S wid William r 1435 N Grand av
Barter Leo J (Barter & Autry) 216 N 7th r 1435 N Grand av
Barter Mary E r 3051 Glasgow pl
Barter S L sec J A Ruhl Clothing Co 905 Washington av
Barter William D carp r 3841 Flad av
Barter & Autry (Leo J Barter and Harry Autry) billiards 216 N 7th
Barteske William woodwkr r 4200 Manchester av
Bartezki Bernard mach r 1301 S 13th
Bartezki Charles polish r 1301 S 13th
Bartezki Emil A billiards 1007 S 11th slot machines 1407 S 7th r 924 Rutger
Bartezki Flora music 1301 S 13th
Bartezki Peter r 1301 S 13th
Bartezki Philip polish r 1301 S 13th
Bartfeld Herman saloon 1132 N 8th r 4184 Morgan
Bartfeld Hyman saloon 901 Biddle
Bartfeld Maud steno Blackwell-Wielandy B & S Co r 4184 Morgan
Bartfeld Minnie steno Broderick & Bascom Rope Co r 4184 Morgan
Bartfeld Paul R shoe r 1502 Biddle
Barth Alfred C tailor 941 N Vandeventer av r 3892 Windsor pl
Barth Amandus lab r 3547 Wisconsin av
Barth Anna r 1710 Hickory
Barth Anna wid Prosper E r 3213 Cass av
Barth Arthur C F butcher r 3329A Iowa av
Barth August S clk Ry Mail Service r 4753 Michigan av
Barth Benjamin A clk r 4753 Michigan av
Barth Caroline wid Christopher r 3133½ St Vincent av
Barth Catherine wid George r 828 N 18th
Barth Catherine wid Mathias r 1945 Hebert
Barth Champ shoe r 2618A Clark av
Barth Charles cab mkr r 3309 Caroline

Top of page 150 of *Gould's St. Louis City Directory* for 1908. Note the four Barselotti wage earners, Allesio, Francesco, Pasquale and Pellegrino. All reside at 2352 Carr St., three working as "laborers" and one, Pasquale, working as "statues." Likely, Pasquale is the father, a master sculptor, teaching his three sons, apprentices. Many immigrant families brought their livelihoods with them from Italy.

synagogues, cemeteries, funeral parlors, railroad lines, fraternal organizations and so forth. Often they contain a city map, as well as numerous business advertisements. In some cases a "reverse directory" is included in the back of the volume; this lists the city's employed inhabitants by street address rather than alphabetically by surname.

City directories enable you to note, year by year, the movement of your ancestors from one address to another; changes in an ancestor's occupation; the age at which children entered the work force; for Roman Catholics, the parish they most likely belonged to; for Jews, their synagogue; for ancestors with a substantial business, an advertisement, perhaps with a picture; an ancestor's neighbors (who frequently turn out to be relatives); and more. The initial appearance of an ancestor's name usually marks the year when he arrived in the city or obtained his first job; the disappearance of the name generally indicates that the ancestor has moved out of the city or died.

When you have a religious record, such as a baptismal or marriage certificate, that provides the name of the officiating clergyman but not the name of the church, you may learn the church by looking the clergyman up in the city directory. The directory will indicate the parish with which he was affiliated, allowing you to pursue your family search in the archives of that parish.

Fortunately for Americans seeking Italian ancestors, city directories are encyclopedic.

Newspapers in English and Italian. Perhaps no single historical source reveals the day-to-day world of your ancestors as vividly and as thoroughly as the local daily or weekly newspaper. It contains an ongoing record of vital information—births, marriages, anniversaries and deaths; local political events, elections, officials and boards; judicial proceedings and decisions; "River News" or "Harbor

Intelligence"; social events, organizations and clubs; legal notices and product and service endorsements; entertainment and amusements; pictures of people, places and events; and lots of advertisements that indicate what products and services were popular, as well as current styles and prices.

Furthermore, the gossip columns of newspapers in rural areas sometimes noted the arrival of Italian immigrants in the vicinity or the appearance of Italian visitors. Society columns in urban newspapers often reported when Italian-American citizens of standing in the community—a restaurant owner, grocer or baker, businessman or lawyer—departed for Italy to visit relatives, and when they returned home again. Even more informative than the English-language press, however, is the Italian-language press.

There were many newspapers printed in Italian in the late nineteenth and early twentieth century in the United States, and you are more likely to find information about your Italian ancestors in one of these than in the English language press. Italian papers focused on matters of interest and importance to the Italian community. A brief death notice for your immigrant ancestor, or a notice of his or her wedding or anniversary, may have appeared in the English newspaper; but chances are you will find a lengthy obituary, or a full description of the nuptial celebration, in the Italian-language newspaper. Or the family may have bypassed the English press altogether and informed only the Italian newspaper. Most advertisements and news reports about and for the Italian community and its businesses and social activities appear in the Italian newspaper, not the English newspaper.

New York City, for example, had at least ten newspapers in Italian, one of which, the *Eco d'Italia* (*Echo of Italy*), was published from 1849 through 1937. Chicago, Cincinnati, Buffalo, St. Louis, Boston, Philadelphia, Baltimore and numerous other smaller cities each had at least one or two Italian-language newspapers. Most of these newspapers are no longer published, and there is no catalog or listing of them all. You must check the libraries of the state and locality where your ancestors lived. Some Italian-American newspapers are available on microfilm.

Start your search at the Internet website of the National Endowment for the Humanities U.S. Newspaper Program, **www.neh.gov/projects/usnp.html**. This program is a national effort among the states and the federal government to locate, catalog and preserve on microfilm newspapers published in the United States from the eighteenth century to the present. Simply click on the state of interest to you, and you'll find contact information for the program representative in that state.

Also, *Newspapers in Microform: United States, 1948–1983*, 2 vols. (Washington, D.C.: Library of Congress, 1984), lists many nineteenth- and twentieth-century Italian language newspapers that were microfilmed and reported to the Library of Congress by libraries across the country between 1948 and 1983.

Finally, the Immigration History Research Center at the University of Minnesota, St. Paul, has been spearheading a program to microfilm Italian language newspapers. For a list of newspapers filmed from 1985 through 1990, see the *Report on the Italian American Newspaper Microfilming Project* (compiled by Timo Riippa) cited in the Bibliography. The report also names the repository that holds the original.

Italians in Italy

Larger research libraries here in the United States also hold an array of works published in Italy that help you learn more about your immigrant forebear's family and lineage . . . *if* you can read Italian. Since you will have to master at least a minimal grasp of Italian to use the old records of Italy, you might as well start taking lessons now, because these published materials in Italian contain many riches but are not available in English.

Dictionaries of Italian Surnames. What does your family name *mean*? DeFelice's *Dizionario dei Cognomi Italiani* (*Dictionary of Italian Surnames*) and Fucilla's *Our Italian Surnames* (this one's in English) explain the possible origin and meaning of Italian family names. They suggest the geographic area of Italy where each name, and its antecedents, derived, and indicate where the name is concentrated today. If you have not yet discovered your ancestors' *comune*, this information may help narrow your research efforts to a particular province, or at least a particular region.

The etymology of your surname also hints at where your family research may eventually lead—Greece, Germany, Austria, France. . . . For example, my own surname, Colletta, may derive from the Greek word *nike*, meaning "victory," and the Italian diminutive suffix *etta*, signifying "little." Colletta, therefore, might be translated as "Little Victory." It predominates in southern-most Italy and the island of Sicily, precisely where Greek colonies thrived in the ancient world.

Onomatology (the study of the origin and history of proper names) is a complex and artful science, and surname dictionaries sometimes propose different interpretations of the same name. The Italian word *colletta* also happens to be a common noun meaning "collection." Furthermore, *colle* means hill, and *etta* is a diminutive suffix, making *colletta*, "little hill." Nevertheless, in old photographs my Colletta ancestors do look Greek!

In addition, by noting those family names that vary only slightly from yours, you are gaining insight into the possible original spelling, or possible variant spellings, of your own name. Cecati, for instance, may have changed to Checati in the United States because in Italian "ce" is pronounced "che." But in earlier centuries the name may have been Cecato, Cecate or Cecata, derived from *cecità*, "blindness." The American genealogist named Checati who has not consulted a surname dictionary might miss the possible link between his own ancestors and the Cecato individuals he keeps coming across in old Italian records.

Italian National Biographies. The *Dizionario Biografico degli Italiani* (*Biographical Dictionary of the Italians*) and *Enciclopedia Biografica e Bibliografica Italiana* (*Italian Biographical and Bibliographical Encyclopedia*) are multivolume sets containing biographical sketches of tens of thousands of Italians who, from the Middle Ages through the twentieth century, distinguished themselves in the arts and humanities, government, diplomacy, military service, science, education and other sectors of Italian life (see illustration on p. 47).

Noting the places of origin of men and women with your family name—whether or not you can place them in your family tree—enables you to surmise where that surname flourished in Italy, and thereby define the geographic parameters of your research.

Furthermore, by noting family names close to your own, you may discover how your surname was spelled in earlier centuries. Or, best of all, searching Italian national biographies might reveal that you do indeed have an ancestor or two who were prominent personages in the Italy of their day.

Genealogies of Titled Families. Numerous genealogies of Italian families may be found in American libraries having extensive genealogical and heraldic collections, such as the New York Public Library (**www.nypl.org**) and the

COMPAGNONI

taria, che il C. fosse ancora attivo nel 1680 (Nagler, 1836; Bénézit) o nel 1700 (Zani; Salerno, *Il vero Filippo...*, 1970), ma già al tempo del De Dominici non si conservava più alcun ricordo della data e del luogo di morte.

FONTI E BIBL.: B. De Dominici, *Vite de' pittori, scultori, ed architetti napoletani*, III, Napoli 1745, pp. 252 s.; J. Füssli, *Allgemeines Künstlerlexikon*, Zürich 1763, p. 134; P. Zani, *Enciclopedia metodica... delle Belle Arti*, I, 7, Parma 1821, pp. 13, 170; G. Nagler, *Neues allgemeines Künstlerlexikon*, III, München 1836, pp. 59-60; A. Berger, *Inventar der Kunstsammlung des Erzherzoges Leopold Willhelm von Österreich*, in *Jahrbuch der Kunsthistorischen Sammlungen des Allerhöchsten Kaiserhauses*, I (1883), p. CVIII; H. Mireur, *Dictionn. des ventes d'art faites en France et à l'étranger pendant les XVIIIme et XIXme siècles*, XII, Paris 1911, p. 236; A. De Rinaldis, *Pinacoteca del Museo naz. di Napoli*, Napoli 1911, p. 427; G. B. D'Addosio, *Documenti ined. di artisti napoletani del XVI e XVII secolo*, in *Arch. stor. per le provcince napol.*, XXXVIII (1913), p. 46; E. Bénézit, *Dictionnaire... des Peintres ...*, I, Paris 1924, p. 992; N. Pevsner, *Die Barockmalerei in den romanischen Ländern*, Potsdam 1928, p. 116; G. Ceci, *Bibliografia per la storia delle arti figurative nell'Italia merid.*, Napoli 1937, pp. 71, 144, 666; R. Causa, *Francesco Nomé detto Monsù Desiderio*, in *Paragone*, VII (1956), 75, p. 39; Id., *Pittura napoletana dal XV al XIX sec.*, Bergamo 1957, p. 54; N. Di Carpegna, *Pittori napoletani del '600 e del '700* (catal.), Roma 1958, pp. 14-15; L. Mortari, *Dipinti della Gall. nazionale a Palazzo Barberini*, in *Boll. d'arte*, s. 4, XLIII (1958), p. 287; A. E. Pérez Sánchez, *Pintura italiana del siglo XVII en España*, Madrid 1965, pp. 384-386; L. Salerno, *Salvator Rosa*, Milano 1965, p. 60; Id., *Il dissenso nella pittura. Intorno a Filippo Napoletano, Caroselli, Salvatore Rosa e altri*, in *Storia dell'arte*, 1970, 5, p. 38; Id., *Il vero Filippo Napoletano e il vero Tassi, ibid.*, 1970, 6, p. 148; R. Causa, *La pittura del Seicento a Napoli dal Naturalismo al Barocco*, in *Storia di Napoli*, V, 2, Napoli 1972, pp. 941, 981 s. nota 107; *Kunsthist. Museum, Wien. Verzeichnis der Gemälde*, Wien 1973, p. 45; M. Marini, *Pittori a Napoli, 1610-1656. Contributi e schede*, Roma 1974, pp. 90-91; L. Salerno, *Precisazione su Filippo Napoletano e i suoi « affini »*, in *Arte illustrata*, VII (1974), 57, p. 43; U. Thieme-F. Becker, *Künstlerlexikon*, VII, p. 282. P. SANTA MARIA

COMPAGNONI, GIUSEPPE. – Nacque a Lugo di Romagna il 3 marzo 1754 da Giovanni e Domenica Ettorri, e fu battezzato col nome di Marco Giuseppe. La famiglia, che risiedeva nel paese da circa due secoli, aveva conosciuto l'agiatezza, ma alcune sfortunate iniziative ne avevano recentemente minato il patrimonio, sicché il C., dopo aver appreso dal padre i primi rudimenti del leggere e dello scrivere, venne avviato alle scuole pubbliche anziché a quelle private, che pure fornivano maggiori garanzie di efficienza. Qui, tra maestri bizzarri e maneschi, dimostrò di possedere fervida curiosità

sorretta da vivace intelligenza: studiò umanità, logica, filosofia e a dodici anni passò al corso superiore di studi, dove poté giovarsi dell'insegnamento del domenicano Cavalletti, professore di teologia. Nel frattempo il padre, che rimasto vedovo si era risposato con Anna Folicaldi (della matrigna il C. conservò sempre un affettuosissimo ricordo), decise di indirizzarlo alla carriera ecclesiastica, a motivo delle spiccate doti di spirito ed ingegno ch'egli dimostrava rispetto agli altri fratelli. Dovette così rinunciare agli studi di giurisprudenza, ai quali si sentiva inclinato, per rivolgersi alla teologia, e in questa facoltà si laureò nel 1778, dopo esser stato ordinato sacerdote dal vescovo di Imola. In seguito però riprese ad occuparsi di diritto e letteratura, alternando i pubblicisti Grozio, Pufendorf, Cumberland e Lampredi ai *philosophes* Montesquieu, Beccaria, Filangieri. La sua franca adesione ai principi dell'illuminismo e l'indipendenza di giudizio con cui manifestò aperta ammirazione per la politica giurisdizionalista e l'opera riformatrice di Giuseppe II gli attirarono però i sospetti degli inquisitori di Bologna e Ferrara; non ne derivò alcun processo, ma il C. perse la possibilità di ottenere una pensione a Roma che gli avrebbe consentito di evadere dal chiuso mondo della provincia per inserirsi in un circuito culturale e politico di ben altro respiro, analogamente a quanto era verificato per il suo coetaneo e conterraneo Vincenzo Monti. All'inizio del 1785 il C. pensò allora di trasferirsi a Venezia, dove la circolazione delle idee sperava di far valere la sua penna, ma il progetto rientrò per la sopravvenuta morte del padre; accettò allora, alla fine di giugno, l'invito di G. Ristori di recarsi a Bologna a dirigere le *Memorie enciclopediche*, settimanale di notizie letterarie, cui riuscì ben presto a dare nuovo impulso con una serie di articoli pubblicati sotto lo pseudonimo di Ligofilo. Ebbe così inizio una fervida – e talvolta frenetica – attività di letterato e poligrafo che il C. continuò fino al termine della sua vita, distinguendosi sempre per la freschezza dello stile, la vivacità lessicale, la disponibilità ad avvicinare una quantità incredibile di questioni e problemi.

Typical page from the *Dizionario Biografico degli Italiani*. The sketch of Giuseppe Compagnoni begins with the facts of his birth and parentage, then proceeds to recount in detail his life as a philosopher, author and editor. The small type above Compagnoni is the list of references (*Fonti e Bibliografia*) that concludes the preceding biography. Each one ends with such a list.

Library of Congress. However, these volumes will not be of immediate use to most Americans, because almost none of them chronicle the *popolino* (common people) who made up the bulk of immigrants to America.

On the contrary, the vast majority of published Italian genealogies document families of the aristocracy, nobility and royalty. It has already been pointed out that in Italy there is little interest in genealogy. Those Italians who do engage in genealogy tend to be men and women descended from ancient families bearing titles and coats of arms.

The genealogies of these illustrious families are usually large and sumptuous works published in the seventeenth, eighteenth and nineteenth centuries, often illustrated with hand-colored heraldic arms. Some, such as Battilana's *Genealogie delle Famiglie Nobili di Genova* (*Genealogies of the Noble Families of Genoa*), focus on the noble families of a particular city, while others, such as Di Casalgerardo's *Nobiliario di Sicilia* (*Book of Nobility of Sicily*), concentrate on the nobility of a particular region. *Contributo alla Bibliografia Genealogica Italiana* (*Contribution to Italian Genealogical Bibliography*), compiled by Antonio Gheno, is an extensive bibliography of published genealogies of ancient and titled families of Italy.

Albo Nazionale: Famiglie Nobili dello Stato Italiano (*National Album: Noble Families of the Italian State*) is a dictionary of titled Italian families bearing arms. The *Libro d'Oro della Nobilità Italiana* (*Golden Book of Italian Nobility*), updated every few years, is a directory of living Italians who hold titles.

Hereditary titles were outlawed in Italy in 1946 when the monarchy was abolished. Today all Italians are equal under the law. Nevertheless, titles continue to be used socially. Also, if the title is legally incorporated into the surname, its use is lawful. For a succinct explanation of Italian nobility, see "A Guide to Italian Heraldry" by Cav. Luigi Mendola in *POINTers*, Vol. 5, No. 4, Winter 1991. (Cav. stands for *Cavaliere*, which means "knight," so the English equivalent would be "Sir.") Sir Luigi Mendola's website is discussed below under "Internet Websites."

If oral tradition has it that your family is a scion of a noble Italian house, published genealogies such as these may prove or disprove the claim. Even if your family has no such tradition, it is still wise to check published genealogies to see whether one with your surname exists. Many a family fortune has been exhausted and "downward mobility" has been far from rare within the Italian nobility (more about Italian titles and terminology in Chapters 4 and 7). So American descendants of poor Italian immigrants do discover sometimes, after climbing a few generations of their family tree, that one branch or another does indeed link up with a noble or royal dynasty.

Maps and Gazetteers. It is impossible to conduct Italian genealogical research without using maps and gazetteers of Italy. The country's internal and external boundaries have been redrawn many times over the centuries, and—as stated earlier—many towns and villages have the same or similar names.

Two major gazetteers available in U.S. libraries list, in alphabetical order, all of the *comuni* and *frazioni* of Italy, together with essential data about each one, including its province, current population, postal code, Catholic diocese and so forth. The *Annuario Generale, Comuni e Frazioni d'Italia* (*General Annual, Towns and Villages of Italy*) is published every five years by the Touring Club Italiano of Milan, and the *Nuovo Dizionario dei Comuni e Frazioni di Comuni* (*New Dictionary of Towns and Villages*) is updated periodically.

Moreover, now you may access an Italian gazetteer on the Internet. An effort is currently underway to create a website for every *comune* of Italy. Simply enter the name of your ancestral *comune* into any browser, and chances are good you will find a site containing the town's history, geography, cultural institutions, tourist attractions, administration and so on. Use the facts you gathered from interviewing relatives and examining materials at home to determine which of the towns with the same name is the right one for *your* family.

The Italian Genealogical Group has announced that it is in the process of making available on its website, **www.italiangen.org/default.stm**, a complete gazetteer of Italy. Some websites already contain partial gazetteers. There are also websites for various regions, such as **http://sicilia.indettaglio.it/ita/index.html** (see illustration on p. 51). This site contains information about each of the 390 *comuni* of Sicily's nine provinces—Agrigento, Caltanisetta, Catania, Enna, Messina, Palermo, Ragusa, Siracusa and Trapani—and it is available in Italian and English. The site **www.circolocalabrese.org** focuses exclusively on researching Calabrian descent.

In 1870 Austria's southern Tyrol became Italy's region of Trentino-Alto Adige. If your family comes from an alpine town of northeastern Italy, therefore, you may need to consult the gazetteer of the Austro-Hungarian Empire, *Allgemeines Geografisches Statistisches Lexikon aller Osterreicheischen Staaten* (*General Geographical and Statistical Lexicon of All Austrian States*), to determine the town's original name. This eleven-volume gazetteer is available on microfilm from the Family History Library (see p. 55). You may also have to pursue your pre-1870 genealogical research in the German-language records of Austria.

Similarly, if your ancestors were Italian citizens but your surname is Slavic, they were probably natives of the province of Trieste. Trieste was transferred from Slovenia to Italy in 1918 as a result of World War I. You may be surprised to

⊚ English Version
⊚ Informa un amico
⊚ Le province siciliane
⊚ I comuni siciliani
⊚ Il Turismo
⊚ La Gastronomia
⊚ Editoria e Musica
⊚ Prodotti locali
⊚ Trasporti
⊚ Inserzionisti
⊚ Controlla il carrello
⊚ Cognomi siciliani
⊚ CAP siciliani

⊚ Pagine più recenti
⊚ Cerca nel sito
⊚ Motori interni
⊚ Mailing List

⊚ Profilo aziendale
⊚ Servizi
⊚ Ricariche banner
⊚ E-mail
⊚ Home

Benvenuti in Sicilia.indettaglio.it !
La Sicilia in dettaglio

Questo è un sito sulla Sicilia e le genti che la abitano.

- Conoscerete questa splendida terra, le sue bellezze incomparabili e gli operatori economici che in essa svolgono la loro quotidiana attività realizzando prodotti unici per qualità e genuinità.

- Troverete informazioni e immagini sulle nove provincie siciliane: Agrigento, Caltanissetta, Catania, Enna, Messina, Palermo, Ragusa, Siracusa e Trapani.

- Per ognuno dei trecentonovanta comuni siciliani vengono trattati il turismo, la gastronomia, i prodotti locali, l'edi video, il sistema dei trasporti e sono presentati gli inserzionisti aderenti circuito per quel comune. È anche possibile registrare gratuitamente la azienda.

- Per reperire le informazioni desiderate presenti all'interno del nostro sit distinte modalità di ricerca: un motore di ricerca a testo libero e diversi tematici disponibili per le categorie Turismo, Gastronomia, Editoria, Pro Inserzionisti, C.A.P e Autolinee.

- È infine possibile iscriversi gratuitamente alla nostra Mailing List per rice informazioni mensili sulle novità e i nuovi servizi del sito.

Realizzato da Reti e Sistemi S.r.l., Via S. Maria di Capua n. 1, Trapani, Italia. © Tutti i diritti son

Home page of the website *La Sicilia in dettaglio* (*Sicily in Detail*). The site contains information about every one of the 390 *comuni* of Sicily. Note the top button on the left links to the "English Version." Click on "Cognomi siciliani" (Sicilian surnames) to get a statistical analysis of where any particular surname appears throughout the island.

learn that your family research will have to be accomplished in records handwritten in a Slavic language. If this is the case, you will need to consult old maps of Slovenia to learn whether the Slavic names of the towns differ from the current Italian names.

Going back even further in time, Italy acquired the island of Sardinia from France in 1767. Most old records of the region of Sardinia are in French.

Perhaps the most detailed atlas available for Italy is the *Grande Carta Topografica del Regno d'Italia* (*Great Topographical Map of the Kingdom of Italy*), first printed by the Istituto Geografico Militare (Military Geographical Institute) in Florence in 1882. It covers the entire Italian peninsula, Sicily and Sardinia in 277 maps at a scale of 1:100,000, all of which were updated and republished periodically into the twentieth century.

These maps show every topographical feature imaginable, including every hill, valley and river; every tiny cluster of houses, large orchards and vineyards; mines, railroads and railroad stations; all thoroughfares, from surfaced highways to footpaths; all bridges, substantial stone walls enclosing estates, convents and monasteries; ruins from antiquity; and more. Rural churches and cemeteries are marked, and villas in the countryside are often identified by family name (see illustration on p. 53.) The Library of Congress has a complete set of the *Grande Carta Topografica del Regno d'Italia*.

If you want the convenience of owning your own atlas and gazetteer of modern Italy, the best one available is *Euro Atlas: Italy*. *Euro Atlas* is a set of volumes encompassing all of the countries of Europe; each volume contains the maps of a different country. The maps show not only roads and highways, but topographical features and political divisions too, and each volume has an extensive alphabetical gazetteer in the back.

Portion of *Grande Carta Topografica* showing Sicilian coast east of the city of Girgenti. Note abundance of detail, including country houses labeled with the names of the families. *(Photocopy of original in the Library of Congress.)*

The *Euro Atlas* is printed in Germany and distributed in the United States by the American Map Corporation, Maspeth, New York. It may be found in larger book and map stores across the country. If you plan to travel in Italy, the *Euro Atlas: Italy* is indispensable.

Italian Local History. Just as there are published histories of American cities, counties and states that genealogists use for the wealth of information they contribute to individual family histories, so too are there published histories of Italian towns, cities, provinces and regions, which prove valuable to Americans researching their ancestry in Italy. Naturally, these are most often written in Italian by Italian historians and are found in larger research libraries with extensive foreign collections, such as the Library of Congress and state and university libraries. They contain a wealth of detail about the families involved in the community's foundation and development, commercial activities and social and religious life.

One typical example is *Casteldaccia nella Storia della Sicilia* (*Casteldaccia in the History of Sicily*), an account of the tiny farming community where my grandfather Santo Colletta was born. Researched and written by the local pastor (the town only has one parish, and the author enjoyed ready access to its archives), this history begins with the earliest mention of Casteldaccia in seventeenth-century records and recounts the town's life to the mid-twentieth century. It chronicles when each new family name first appears in the records, describes the composition and actions of the town council, and explains the community's involvement in larger historical events, such as the Risorgimento and World War I.

One of the thirty-three families residing in Casteldaccia when its parish was founded in 1727 was the Colletta family. So humble were the Collettas, however, that they appear only three times in this 295-page book.

The only way to know whether such a history exists for your forebears' community is to search diligently with the help of librarians in larger research libraries and online.

More broadly accessible than town histories are histories of provinces and regions. *I Sette Re di Agrigento* (*The Seven Kings of Agrigento*), for example, not only relates the history of a Sicilian province, but includes a clear description of the organization and contents of the *archivio di stato* (state archives) in the *capo luogo*, Agrigento. The book concludes with a list of the 688 *notai* (notaries) who worked in the notarial district of Agrigento between 1486 and 1859, and the 507 *notai* who worked in the notarial district of Sciacca between 1434 and 1875, with the years each was licensed. (Notaries and the importance of the records they created will be discussed in Chapter 4.)

A work such as Giosue Musca's two-volume *Storia della Puglia* (*The History of Apulia*) covers the geographical, historical, political, social, economic and cultural development of an entire five-province *regione*. Provincial and regional histories do not provide the same amount of personal and familial detail that town histories do, though you may still find information about your ancestors if they participated in any way in provincial or regional affairs.

Moreover, a great deal of Italian local history is now available on the Internet, both in English and Italian. Websites already cited in the section "Maps and Gazetteers" contain local history, as do some of the websites discussed in "Internet Websites," below.

The Family History Library

The Family History Library in Salt Lake City (hereafter referred to as the FHL) warrants special mention, as it is the largest genealogical library in the world and contains an extensive collection of resources on microfilm for researching Italian ancestry. Although the FHL is owned and maintained for religious reasons by The Church of Jesus Christ of Latter-day Saints, its use by the general public is graciously encouraged, and thousands of Family History Centers located around the world make accessing the FHL's microfilm easy.

You may search the FHL's catalog online by family name, place name or record type at any Family History Center or on your own computer at **www.familysearch.org**. Then you may borrow any roll of microfilm you choose. Simply submit your request at a Family History Center (there is a modest fee to cover postage) and the microfilm will be sent from Salt Lake City to that particular Center, where you may view it for a period of three weeks before it is returned. Here is just a sampling of some of the FHL's many useful materials for Italian genealogy.

Instructions and Glossaries. The FHL's website provides excellent instructional materials. A "Research Outline for Italian Genealogy" describes the various types of Italian records that have been created over the centuries. A "Glossary of Italian Words" and "Glossary of Latin Words" contain the terms you are most likely to encounter in genealogical sources and give their English equivalents. Both glossaries will prove indispensable when it comes time to decipher the old Italian records of your ancestors.

You may print out a hard copy of any FHL research aid. Or you may purchase them for a nominal price at Family History Centers or by writing: Family History Library, North West Temple Street, Salt Lake City, Utah 84150.

Microfilmed Italian Records. Since the early 1980s the FHL has microfilmed millions of original records of genealogical value in Italian archives. Chances are excellent that at least some of the birth, marriage and death records of your ancestral *comuni* have been filmed.

However, even if you discover that the FHL has not yet filmed any records of your ancestors' towns, it is still a good idea to borrow and examine several rolls of microfilm for any town in the vicinity. This exercise serves two purposes: (1) it familiarizes you with the sources available in that part of Italy, what they look like, what information they contain, etc.; and (2) it introduces you to the script you will encounter when you do eventually access the records of your ancestors (now begins your training in paleography!).

Databases. Also searchable at the FHL's website are several enormous databases compiled by volunteers of The Church of Jesus Christ of Latter-day Saints. One is the International Genealogical Index (IGI), which contains over 485,000 Italian names extracted from original birth and marriage records. An important part of preparing to use Italian records is to search the IGI for the surnames you will be researching in Italy. You may not find any of your ancestors in the IGI. On the other hand, you may, because the record of their birth or marriage just happened to appear in one of the civil or sacramental registers selected for inclusion in the database.

One advantage of the IGI is the way it groups like-sounding names together. By consulting it, you may uncover variant spellings of your surname you would not otherwise think of. The IGI, therefore, is a tool you should not overlook, especially since it is constantly being expanded, and more and more Italian names appear in each new edition.

Form Letters. One very useful feature of the FHL website, particularly if you have little knowledge of Italian, is the form letters for obtaining records from Italian repositories. The letters are in Italian, but blank spaces are left for you to fill in the names, dates and places of the ancestors you are researching. Correspondence will be discussed further in Chapter 7.

Much more information about the collections, services and publications of the FHL is available at **www.familysearch.org**. Besides the sampling highlighted above, the FHL holds a wealth of material relevant to Italian genealogy, including microfilm copies of many of the published works already discussed, as well as most of the federal, state and local records of the United States described in Chapter 3. Do not neglect to take full advantage of the extraordinary hospitality of The Church of Jesus Christ of Latter-day Saints.

Private Repositories with Italian Collections

Several major research centers in the United States hold substantial collections of materials relating to Italian immigration and Italian-American history. For instance, the Immigration History Research Center at the University of Minnesota in St. Paul (**www.umn.edu/ihrc**) contains an Italian-American collection composed of about 1,400 items, including not only standard published works in the field of Italian immigration history, but also unpublished dissertations and many books, tracts and pamphlets printed in Italian by immigrant presses. The archives of the Order of the Sons of Italy in America is housed there, as is a substantial collection of microfilmed American newspapers in the Italian language from communities across the country (already mentioned under "Newspapers in English and Italian"). For guides to the Italian-American collection in the Immigration History Research Center, see the "Research Aids" section of the Bibliography.

Another example is the archives of the Knights of Columbus (**www.kofc.org**), a Catholic fraternal and philanthropic organization of which many Italian Americans have been members. The collection includes correspondence, pamphlets, publications, programs, newspaper clippings and books relating to the history of the order.

Internet Websites

A number of pertinent websites have already been cited, including those for the Library of Congress, Family History Library, Allen County Public Library, New York Public Library, the National Endowment for the Humanities U.S. Newspaper Program, Sicily, Calabria and the three major Italian genealogical societies. However, there are *hundreds* of World Wide Web sites that may be useful for researching your Italian ancestry. It all depends on who your ancestors were, where they resided and what kind of lives they led.

A good place to start your search is by clicking on the suggested "links" on the site of the Italian Genealogical Group, **www.italiangen.org/default.stm**. Another possible starting point is **www.cyndislist.com**, which links to many sites relevant to Italian genealogical research. Or, if you prefer, simply type "Italian genealogy" into any Internet search engine (Excite, Yahoo, Google, etc.), then cull through the hundreds of hits one by one. What follows is a tiny representative sampling of some of the most helpful websites.

Italian Genealogy Homepage (**http://italiangenealogy. tardio.com/html**). The work of Louis Mendola, this site contains informative essays in English on various aspects of conducting genealogical research in the records of Italy. The information is useful, and there are sample letters too.

Ancestry.com (**www.ancestry.com**). This mammoth site contains hundreds of databases and much useful information, including extensive original records. The *free* Social Security Death Index lists 1.5 million persons who had

Social Security numbers and whose deaths were reported to the Social Security Administration between 1937 and 1962, and 38 million persons whose deaths were reported between 1962 and 1988 (see the article by Sharon DeBartolo Carmack cited in the Bibliography). Other parts of Ancestry.com—such as all U.S. censuses, 1790 through 1930, with indexes—are accessible for a monthly fee.

The Universal Currency Converter (**www.xe.com/ucc**). This site is a currency converter; it will convert dollars into euros and vice-versa. Very handy!

American Family Immigration History Center (**www.ellis islandrecords.org**). (See illustration on p. 61.) This site contains digitized images of the passenger arrival records of New York, 1892–1924, and a search engine for finding one passenger among the estimated twenty-two million names.

Italian Ancestry (**www.ItalianAncestry.com**). This site links to numerous others categorized under "Italian Genealogy Web Sites," "Italia in General," "Writing to Italy," "Tool Box," "United States," "Italians in America," "International Italiano" and "General Subjects."

Virgilio (**www.virgilio.it**). Italian telephone directories are searchable at this site. If you know the region where an ancestor was born, but not the exact province or town, you might consult phone books to see where your family name is concentrated, and then proceed to search the records of that province or town (as described in Chapters 4 and 5). In Italy you will find a full set of telephone books in all airports and major train stations; the Library of Congress has a set, and the FHL has them on microfilm.

Many more useful World Wide Web addresses will be given in Chapters 3–7.

Sign In | Regis

Screen:

ELLIS ISLAND ON-LINE

▶ Foundation Membership
▶ Your Account

LIBERTY ELLIS ISLAND

192.168.4.69 ▶ PASSENGER SEARCH ▶ GIFT SHOP ▶ FAMILY SCRAPBOOKS ▶ YOUR ELLIS ISLAND FILE ▶ IMMIGRANT EX

SEARCH IMMIGRATION RECORDS

Enter immigrant's name here

First Name(Optional)   Last Name

SEARCH

ADD A NAME TO THE WALL OF HONOR®

Inscribe a name on the American Immigrant Wall of Honor at Ellis Island. Find out more.

BECOME A MEMBER

Join the Statue of Liberty-Ellis Island Foundation. Only $45/year
— Create and maintain your Family History Scrapbook
— Free printpout and discounts
— Support the work of the Statue of Liberty-Ellis Island Foundation

More Info   Join Now

THE FAMILY HISTORY GIFT SHOP

See the items in our shop

OFFICIAL SPONSORS

LIBERTY ELLIS ISLAND
TM 1992, 1997 THE STATUE OF LIBERTY-
ELLIS ISLAND FOUNDATION, INC.

THE CHURCH OF JESUS CHRIST OF LATTER-DAY SAINTS   *hp*   DISCOVER CARD   AMERICA Online   ORACLE Kodak

Recently redesigned home page of **www.ellisislandrecords.org,** website of the American Family Immigration History Center, a stupendous achievement for immigrant research. The site allows you to search through the lists of passengers and crew members arriving at the port of New York, 1892–1924—approximately 22 million names—in a matter of minutes, then examine any passenger's manifest in digitized form.

3. Key Records in the United States

At this point in your quest to rediscover your Italian heritage, you have taken full advantage of the many published materials available in libraries and on the Internet. You have gathered sufficient information to delve successfully into original historical sources. The vast and fascinating universe of public and private records—federal, state and local—awaits you.

Federal Records

Federal records—records created by departments, agencies and bureaus of the United States government—constitute a major source for all American genealogy. The following overview highlights ways in which federal records may be of particular value with regards to searching for ancestors from Italy. Remember, if you are to continue your family tree climbing in Italian records, you must first learn those three fundamental facts about your immigrant ancestor discussed in Chapter 1.

For more complete information about the records discussed here and other federal records, consult the *Guide to Genealogical Research in the National Archives* cited in the Bibliography or visit **www.archives.gov**, the official website of the National Archives and Records Administration, where an even more detailed guide is available online.

Censuses. The U.S. government has taken a census of the country's population every ten years since 1790. These censuses form the backbone of American genealogy. The information they contain allows researchers to reconstruct the multi-generational skeleton of their family trees.

For Americans of Italian descent, the 1900, 1910, 1920 and 1930 population censuses are particularly helpful, as very few Italian immigrants appear in earlier enumerations (the 1890 census was destroyed by fire). In addition, these censuses provide a date of immigration for residents born overseas and indicate whether the resident was naturalized. Earlier censuses do not contain this information.

The 1910 census illustrated on page 65 shows how wonderfully informative these enumerations can be. Joseph Geraci and his wife (here called Jennie, an American nickname for Giovanna) emigrated from Italy in 1898 with their daughter, then proceeded to have five more healthy children in Haverstraw, New York. Joseph and Jennie did their best to maintain the ancient tradition for naming their children. The eldest daughter is named Jennie after Joseph's mother, Giovanna, and the eldest son is named Samuel after Joseph's father, Santo. The second daughter is named Annie after Jennie's mother, Anna, and the second son is named Joseph after Jennie's father, Giuseppe.

Joseph operates a bakery that he rents (but will own soon), and he has conscientiously secured U.S. citizenship. This immigrant entrepreneur is making the most of the opportunities America has to offer! Notice that this businessman, who deals with government agencies and the general public, can speak English, while his wife, who works at home, cannot. Note, too, that the four Italian aliens working for Joseph reside in the Geraci household. Chances are good they are relatives or *paesani* (former neighbors, fellow countrymen), and that it was Joseph's offer of employment that lured them to America. The three bakers cannot speak English, but the driver who gets out of the bakery and delivers the bread in the neighborhood can.

Federal Census of 1910 for Haverstraw, Rockland County, New York, showing Geraci family on lines 51–62. Immigration and citizenship data are given in columns 15 and 16. Note that the immigrant who arrived in 1898, Joseph Geraci, is doing well enough in his bakery business by 1910 to employ four recent immigrants from Italy—a typical situation. (*Photograph courtesy of the Latter-day Saints Family History Library.*)

This 1910 census, while itemizing the personal facts particular to the Geracis, reveals that the family was typical of many Italian-American families of that era.

If your ancestors were living in the United States by 1900, 1910, 1920 or 1930, the immigration and citizenship information in a federal census will help lead the way to their ships' passenger lists and naturalization records, and to continued research in Italy—unless, of course, your ancestors just happened to be on a return trip to *la patria* the day the census enumerator came calling. Bear in mind, too, that census information is notoriously inaccurate and should be verified whenever possible by consulting other sources.

Federal censuses are available on microfilm at the National Archives in Washington, D.C., the fourteen Regional Archives (see list below) and numerous libraries around the country, including the FHL. They have also been digitized and uploaded to Internet websites accessible through paid subscription. The 1900 and 1920 censuses are fully indexed by individual personal name. However, the 1910 index covers only twenty-one states, and only ten states of the 1930 census are fully indexed (two states are partially indexed). To find your ancestors in the 1910 and 1930 censuses, therefore, you may need to know the township in which they resided, or their exact street address if they lived in a major city.

The National Archives and Its Regional Archives

National Archives and Records
Administration
700 Pennsylvania Avenue, NW
Washington, DC 20408
(called "Archives 1," it holds the
records of greatest genealogical value)

National Archives at College Park
8601 Adelphi Road
College Park, MD 20740-6001
(called "Archives 2")

National Archives—Northeast Region
Frederick C. Murphy Federal Center
380 Trapelo Road
Waltham, MA 02452-6399
(serves CT, ME, MA, NH, RI
and VT)

National Archives—Northeast Region
201 Varick Street
New York, NY 10014-4811
(serves NJ, NY, PR and VI)

National Archives—Northeast
Region
10 Conte Drive
Pittsfield, MA 01201-8230
(microfilm only; no original records)

National Archives—Mid-Atlantic
Region
900 Market Street
Philadelphia, PA 19107-4292
(serves DE, PA, MD, VA and WV—
archival records)

National Archives—Mid-Atlantic
Region
14700 Townsend Road
Philadelphia, PA 19154-1096
(serves DE, PA, MD, VA and WV—
retired records)

National Archives—Great Lakes
Region
7358 South Pulaski Road
Chicago, IL 60629-5898
(serves IL, IN, MI, MN, OH and
WI)

National Archives—Southeast
Region
1557 St. Joseph Avenue
East Point, GA 30344-2593
(serves AL, GA, FL, KY, MS, NC, SC
and TN)

National Archives—Central Plains
Region
2312 East Bannister Road
Kansas City, MO 64131-3011
(serves IO, KS, MO and NE)

National Archives—Southwest
Region
501 West Felix Street, Building 1
Fort Worth, TX 76115-3405
(serves AR, LA, OK and TX)

National Archives—Rocky Mountain
Region
Bldg. 48, Denver Federal Center
West 6th Avenue and Kipling Street
Denver, CO 80225-0307
(serves CO, MT, ND, NM, SD, UT
and WY)

National Archives—Pacific Region
1000 Commodore Drive
San Bruno, CA 94066-2350
(serves northern CA, HI, NV [except
Clark County], the Pacific Trust
Territories and American Samoa)

National Archives—Pacific Region
24000 Avila Road
1st Floor, East Entrance
Laguna Niguel, CA 92677-3497
(serves AZ; the southern CA
counties of Imperial, Inyo, Kern, Los
Angeles, Orange, Riverside, San
Bernadino, San Diego, San Luis
Obispo, Santa Barbara and Ventura;
and Clark County, NV)

National Archives—Pacific Alaska
Region
6125 Sand Point Way, NE
Seattle, WA 98115-7999
(serves ID, OR and WA)

National Archives—Pacific Alaska
Region
654 West Third Avenue
Anchorage, AK 99501-2145
(serves Alaska)

Passenger Arrival Records. Since 1820 the federal government has kept a record of all passengers arriving on ships at U.S. ports. These passenger lists (sometimes called manifests) contain a wealth of personal data about immigrants who entered the United States through 1957. Particularly noteworthy is that beginning in 1906 these records provided the precise town of birth for every passenger, while earlier lists indicated only "nationality" or "country of origin" or "last permanent residence."

If your immigrant ancestor came in 1906 or later, therefore, here is where you can learn the name of your ancestral *comune!* Bear in mind, however, that the data contained on ships' manifests is often inaccurate or spelled capriciously. Always take this into account when using them in your family research.

Perhaps the busiest port of arrival for Italian immigrants in the 1870s and 1880s was New Orleans. Some of the new arrivals stayed in the Crescent City. Others settled on farm land in rural Louisiana and Mississippi. Still others chose to continue up the Mississippi River and open markets for fresh fruits and vegetables in Baton Rouge, Natchez, Vicksburg, Memphis, Saint Louis and other cities where river commerce ensured brisk business. This settlement pattern explains the concentration of Italian Americans still residing in those areas today.

By the 1890s, though, the vast majority of Italian immigrants were arriving at the ports of New York, Boston, Philadelphia and Baltimore, where their numbers swelled to record highs in the early years of the twentieth century. Most of these were laborers with no particular skill or trade, so entrepreneurship was much more limited among them than it had been among the Italians who had arrived earlier in the South.

Many of these Italian laborers remained in the "Little Italys" of New York, Boston, Philadelphia and Baltimore. Others moved on to employment opportunities in heavy industry and manufacturing in northern cities such as Buffalo and Pittsburgh, where they also formed their own community. Still others gravitated to the coal mines of Pennsylvania and West Virginia.

During the first decade of the twentieth century, Italians in considerable numbers also arrived at New Bedford, Massachusetts, and settled in Rhode Island. In the South, the port of Galveston, Texas, received large numbers of Italians who made their homes throughout the Lone Star State. Ports on the Great Lakes, such as Duluth and Milwaukee, Detroit, Chicago and Cleveland, constituted the major point of entry for Italians immigrating into the U.S. via Canada. (The U.S. government began keeping a record of people crossing the Canadian border in 1895. These lists name only non-Canadians, however, so Italians who immigrated to Canada and became Canadian citizens before entering the United States do not appear on them. The lists are almost identical to ships' manifests, and they are available through 1954.) Many of the Italian laborers who entered the country at Great Lakes ports went to work in the mines of Minnesota's iron range; others ended up in the copper and silver mines of Colorado. San Francisco remained the major Pacific Coast port of arrival for Italians headed for the vineyards of California and the cattle ranches of the Northwest.

The passenger list on page 70 illustrates the broad informational content of U.S. arrival records in the early twentieth century, when immense numbers of Italians were sailing to America. The S.S. *Re d'Italia* entered New York harbor from Palermo, Sicily, on March 10, 1910. Lines 17–20 of her manifest, which have been annotated heavily by U.S. immigration officials at Ellis Island, show the Anselmo family headed for Youngstown, Ohio.

Francesco Anselmo, a 29-year-old workman, and his wife, Anna Scaduto, 22, have been to the United States before. From 1899 through 1907 they resided in Youngstown, where Francesco's mother lives, and where their three-year-old son, Antonio, was born. However, their one-year-old son, Vincenzo, was born in his parents' native Bagheria, Sicily.

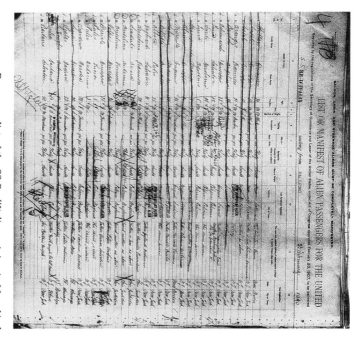

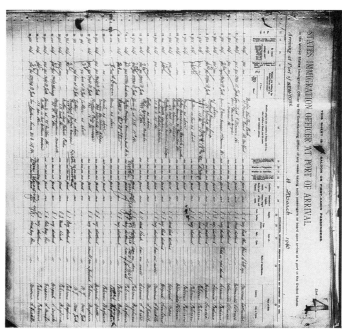

Passenger list of the SS *Re d'Italia*, arriving in New York on 10 March 1910, showing the Anzelmo family on lines 17–20. Note the numerous notations and corrections made by the clerk at Ellis Island (including for Francesco Anzelmo—"Probate Court Geauga Co. Ohio Nov. 7, 1904") to clarify citizenship status of each member of an immigrant family returning to the United States after a sojourn in Italy. (*Photograph courtesy of the Latter-day Saints Family History Library.*)

The data disclose a familiar story. The Anselmos immigrated to the United States, then returned to Sicily, then came back again. Further research would show that Francesco's family included numerous "birds of passage." Immigration officials in New York evidently needed to verify Francesco's citizenship status before admitting his family. They wired the probate court of Geauga County, Ohio, to confirm that Francesco had been naturalized there on November 7, 1904. As soon as confirmation arrived, the Anselmos were admitted, and this time they stayed for good.

Since passenger lists were prepared at the port of embarkation, your ancestor's name will appear as he or she pronounced it, or perhaps as it was written in your ancestor's passport. Do not be surprised if it differs from the surname you use today, especially if your ancestor sailed from a port outside of Italy (where non-Italian speakers would have created the record). In the records of Italy, Francesco Anselmo's family name is consistently spelled Anzelmo, with a "z," not an "s." As already noted in Chapter 1, Italian surnames have changed for many reasons. Finding your ancestor's arrival record, therefore, may turn out to be crucial for learning what surname you will be tracing in the records of Italy.

Did you notice that Francesco's wife, Anna (her nickname was Anichia, which might be translated as Annie), appears on the passenger list under her maiden name, Scaduto? Women in Italy (as well as in France) have always conducted official business under their own family name, not their husband's, and this custom is reflected in the manifests of the steamships of those two countries. If an Italian ancestress of yours came to the United States on a French or Italian liner, she will usually appear in the manifest under her maiden name.

On occasion, though, if she was traveling with her husband, she will appear with *his* surname. An Italian woman with children coming to join her husband in the United States is listed under her maiden name, but the children are listed with their father's surname.

Passenger arrival records for all U.S. ports and Canadian border crossings, as well as alphabetical name indexes to many of them, are available on microfilm at the National Archives and its Regional Archives, FHL, and some public libraries with large genealogical collections. Extensive indexes published in book form are also found in libraries.

Some arrival records have been transcribed onto CD-ROMs, others (notably **www.ellisislandrecords.org**) have been digitized and uploaded to Internet websites. For comprehensive instruction on how to find the passenger lists of the ships that brought your ancestors to America, see *They Came in Ships: A Guide to Finding Your Immigrant Ancestor's Arrival Record*, cited in the Bibliography.

Naturalization Records. The legal process by which Italian immigrants became citizens of the United States could be effected in any federal, territorial, state or local court, and resulted in the creation of a public record. Naturalization laws are complex and have been revised and amended over the years. To summarize in a few words, however, for most immigrants the procedure had two steps: (1) After residing in the United States for two consecutive years, the alien would go to any court of record and declare his or her intention to become a citizen; and (2) after two more years of residency in the United States, the alien would return to any court of record with a U.S. citizen or two to vouch for his or her good moral character and lack of criminal record, and petition for naturalization. Two records, therefore, were created: (1) the declaration of intention and (2) the petition for naturalization.

However, immigrants who arrived under the age of eighteen and remained in this country two years past their twenty-first birthday did not have to file a declaration; they could petition in one step. In addition, prior to 1922 the wife and minor children (under eighteen) of a naturalized citizen gained their "derivative citizenship" through him; that is, they automatically became U.S. citizens, with no paperwork whatsoever.

The declaration and petition both contain biographical facts about the immigrant, although often very few. The records vary tremendously from one court to another, one decade to another, one state or territory to another. Sometimes they include the name of the immigrant's ship, as well as his or her port and date of arrival. Sometimes they mention the name and age of the wife and minor children too.

You may find that your ancestor's name in the naturalization record differs from his or her name on the passenger list. This is because it was during the first few years in America—between arriving in the country and petitioning for citizenship—that surnames often changed. If you cannot find your forebear's ship manifest, it may be because he or she appears under a different surname than the one your family uses today. In such cases the naturalization record sometimes indicates what the original name was.

Unfortunately, though, naturalization records do not always provide the name of the immigrant's ship, or the port and date of arrival, or the name and age of his wife and minor children. Generally, records created after the first decade of the twentieth century tend to be more informative. Moreover, not all immigrants became U.S. citizens. Many declared their intention, but never petitioned; others remained alien residents their entire lives.

The declaration of intention on page 74 and petition for naturalization on page 75 illustrate how rich in family his-

A typical declaration of intention of the early twentieth century. Luciano Basone lived in the United States almost fourteen years (1896 to 1910) before initiating the naturalization process. Many Italian immigrants expected to work only temporarily in America, then return to their native *paese*. Some did indeed do that. Most, however, eventually decided to stay and make a new life for their families here. (*Photocopied document courtesy of Alvie L. Davidson.*)

Typical petition for naturalization from the early twentieth century. Considered in conjunction with his declaration of intention, this document reveals how extensively Luciano Basone and his family traveled before settling down. They arrived at New Orleans in 1896, were in Chicago by 1910, then migrated down to rural Florida in 1912, where Luciano finally found his dream: his own farm. (*Photocopied document courtesy of Alvie L. Davidson.*)

tory naturalization records can be. Luciano Basone, born in Alimena, Italy, in 1854, married Jennie, who had been born in Villarosa, where the couple had six children: Salvatore, 1882; Antonia, 1885; Francis, 1887; Sam, 1889; Carl, 1891; and Rosa, 1893. The two elder children died in Villarosa. Luciano, not unlike a majority of his fellow countrymen, was short and stocky, but his eyes were blue.

On October 31, 1896, Luciano and Jennie Basone and their four children sailed from Naples on board the S.S. *Belaview* and arrived in New Orleans on November 22. The family then traveled to Chicago, very likely by railroad, where Luciano, a laborer, declared his intention to become a U.S. citizen in 1910. Two years later, however, the Basones made their way down to Florida, where Luciano, now claiming his occupation as "Laborer and Farmer," petitioned for naturalization in 1917.

Notice that Luciano, typical of Italian immigrants, did not begin the naturalization process as soon as he might have; he waited almost fourteen years before declaring. At that time he signed with an "x." Nor did he petition as soon as he might have. He only completed the legal procedure in 1917. By that time Luciano had learned to sign his name, but was "able to speak the English language" only "a little bit." Here was one *campagnuolo* (countryman) who managed to escape a dismal existence of oppressive drudgery in a Chicago factory (not to mention the biting winters) for an outdoor agricultural life in a climate more akin to what he had known in his Mediterranean homeland.

Naturalization records made in federal and territorial courts are available at the National Archives or one of its Regional Archives. Naturalizations made in state courts are found in the state archives or library, or the county courthouse where the petition for citizenship was made. Naturalizations made in municipal courts are generally preserved in the city archives. Since September 27, 1906 (when the agency that would become the Immigration and Naturalization Service was created), a copy of all naturalization records made in all courts—federal, territorial, state and municipal—has been filed with the Immigration and Naturalization Service (425 I Street NW, Washington, DC 20536), which maintains a master index. Furthermore, numerous published indexes and finding aids for locating naturalization records may be found in libraries.

The National Archives has microfilmed card indexes to naturalizations filed in many courts around the country. These indexes are arranged by surname in alphabetical order and provide sufficient information to locate the original naturalization record. Most of them cover a single U.S. district or circuit court; however, a few of them index naturalizations made in state and local courts as well. For example, one index of particular value for Italian Americans covers all naturalizations made in federal, state and local courts of New York, 1792–1906. All of these microfilmed indexes are also available through the FHL.

For further information see Loretto Dennis Szucs' *They Became Americans* and Christina Schaefer's *Guide to Naturalization Records of the United States*, both cited in the Bibliography. Note, however, that Schaefer's guide is far from exhaustive; use it judiciously. It appears to include only those records that have been microfilmed by The Church of Jesus Christ of Latter-day Saints. Many counties known to have naturalization records do not appear at all in this work.

Passport Applications. Prior to 1941, except for brief periods during the Civil War and immediately after World War I, passports were not required for Americans to travel overseas or re-enter the United States. Some Americans applied for and received a passport; others did not bother. Italians who became U.S. citizens and then returned to Italy to visit relatives or bring back a wife and children frequently carried only their certificate of naturalization with them or, as we have seen in the case of Francesco Anselmo, not even that.

One advantage of locating a passport application for a naturalized citizen is that it contains the date and court of naturalization. It may also state the exact date and place of birth of the applicant and his wife and minor children. Applications since 1914 also contain the applicant's photograph and his or her immediate travel plans, including the "reason for return" to Italy. Given the history of Italian immigration, and particularly the "birds of passage" phenomenon, a passport application—if your immigrant ancestor applied for one—could help you secure the facts you need to continue your research in the records of Italy.

The 1904 passport application of Vincenzo Abbattiello is illustrated on page 79. It shows when and where he was born, names the ship that brought him to America and his port of debarkation, specifies the court and date of his naturalization, and provides a physical description of the man. Vincenzo is a merchant who intends to remain abroad two full years, but the reason for the long stay overseas is not given.

Passport applications from 1791 through 1925, as well as registers and indexes to help you find one application in particular, are available on microfilm through the National Archives and FHL. Applications since 1926 are still held by the Passport Office of the U.S. Department of State.

Other Federal Records. Other federal records—for instance, World War I Draft Registration Cards, which are accessible on microfilm at the National Archives and the FHL—may also be useful in preparing to find and use Italian records. It all depends on the activities of your immigrant ancestor. Each one's story is unique. Different sources are helpful for different individuals.

40.—Application for Passport.—Naturalized Citizen.
[EDITION OF JULY, 1888.]

John Polhemus Printing Company, Printers and Mf'g Stationers, 121 Fulton St., New York

No. 95018

Issued NOV 3 1904

United States of America.

STATE OF *New York*
COUNTY OF *Kings* } ss:

I, *Vincenzo Abbattiello* a NATURALIZED AND LOYAL CITIZEN OF THE UNITED STATES, do hereby apply to the Department of State at Washington for a passport for myself ~~and wife, and my minor children as follows:~~ born at *Italy* on the *2* day of *February 1852* and

In support of the above application, I do solemnly swear that I was born at *Maddaloni* in *Italy* on or about the *21* day of *February* 18*52*; that I emigrated to the United States, sailing on board the *California*, from *Naples*, on or about the *30th* day of *March*, 18*90*; that I resided *14* years, uninterruptedly, in the United States, from *1890 to 1904* at *New York*; that I was naturalized as a citizen of the United States before the *County* Court of *Westchester* at *New York*, on the *30th* day of *October 1903*, as shown by the accompanying Certificate of Naturalization; that I am the IDENTICAL PERSON described in said Certificate; that I am domiciled in the United States, my permanent residence being at *New York*, in the State of *N.Y.* where I follow the occupation of *merchant*; that I am about to go abroad temporarily; and that I intend to return to the United States *two years*, with the purpose of residing and performing the duties of citizenship therein.

OATH OF ALLEGIANCE.

Further, I do solemnly swear that I will support and defend the Constitution of the United States against all enemies, foreign and domestic; that I will bear true faith and allegiance to the same; and that I take this obligation freely, without any mental reservation or purpose of evasion; So HELP ME GOD.

Sworn to before me, this *2nd* day of *November* 190*4*

Vincenzo Abbatiello

Joseph Sessa
Com. of Deeds

DESCRIPTION OF APPLICANT.

Age: *52* years.
Stature: *5* feet, *3* inches, Eng.
Forehead: *high*
Eyes: *Brown*
Nose: *regular*

Mouth: *regular*
Chin: *pointed*
Hair: *Black*
Complexion: *light*
Face: *oval*

IDENTIFICATION.

Bkly — Nov 2, 1904

I hereby certify that I know the above-named *Vincenzo Abbattiello* personally, and know him to be the identical person referred to in the within described Certificate of Naturalization, and that the facts stated in his affidavit are true to the best of my knowledge and belief.

Frank DeMaio
64 Degraw H.

[ADDRESS OF WITNESS.]

Applicant desires passport sent to following address:

Vincenzo Abbattiello
c/o Sessa
40 Union St
Brooklyn
N.Y.

One dollar tax, as imposed by law, will be required, in U. S. currency, with each application. When husband, wife, minor children and servants expect to travel together, a single passport for the whole will suffice. For any other person in the party a separate passport will be required. Address " Department of State, Passport Division," Washington, D. C.

U.S. passport application of Vincenzo Abbattiello, dated 2 November 1904. Note that the complete facts of the alien's immigration and naturalization history are supplied. (*Photograph courtesy of the Latter-day Saints Family History Library.*)

State Records

Federal records are not the only sources to turn to for the basic facts about your immigrant ancestor. Records kept on the state level may also prove useful. Located in every state capital, sometimes together in the same building, sometimes in two separate buildings, are a state archives and a state library. What these agencies are called differs from state to state—for instance, there's the Mississippi Department of Archives and History, The Library of Virginia, the Pennsylvania State Archives and Pennsylvania State Library, and many other variations. It is in these agencies that you will find the historical records created by that state's government, as well as other materials, published and manuscript, for researching the history and people of that state.

Moreover, in addition to the state-run archives and library, many states have an entirely separate, non-governmental organization called the "state historical society," which also houses published and manuscript resources pertinent to the history of the state. There, too, you may find official state records or copies of them.

Highlighted here are ways in which specific state records may be particularly helpful for tracing Italian immigrants.

Censuses. Most states enumerated their populations at some time or other. State censuses complement the federal censuses already discussed, because they were often taken in years *between* federal censuses. Combining information from the two, therefore, better establishes the chronology of an Italian family, showing moves that were made, and family members who died or moved away, between visits from the U.S. census taker.

State censuses frequently indicate how long each resident has been living in the state, and the year when foreign-born residents first arrived in the country. Citizenship status is also often indicated, narrowing the time frame in which you might search for a declaration of intention or petition for naturalization. Some New York State censuses even give the *place* of naturalization.

Remember, Italian "birds of passage" came to America once, twice or more before bringing their wives and children and establishing their permanent home here. Even then, many Italian families, particularly those who resided in cities, moved from one address to another several times during their first few years in the United States. It is easy to see how state censuses might "fill in" family history missing from the federal censuses.

A state census may also serve as a substitute for the missing 1890 federal census (the one destroyed by fire). New York State, for example, conducted two enumerations around that time—one in 1885, the other in 1892—which "fill in the gap."

In addition, Italian families often played host to new immigrants for brief periods of time—as we noted in the Geraci household of 1910. A "bird of passage" might reside with a cousin, in-law, uncle or *paesano* for a year or two, or maybe for just a few months, until he was financially able to move into a place of his own and send for his family. When these brief stays did not happen to fall in years when a U.S. census taker came around, no federal enumeration records them. But censuses taken on the state level in the "off years" may capture such a temporary sojourn.

Original state census schedules are generally kept in the state archives, library or historical society. Many have been microfilmed, however, and are easily accessible through the FHL and local libraries. Name indexes to virtually every census make searching them a manageable undertaking.

Vital Records. Every state has a statewide agency—most were established between 1880 and 1912—for recording births, marriages, divorces and deaths. The birth records of your immigrant ancestor's children may help establish what the family's original name was. The immigrant's death certificate may indicate the town or province or region where he or she was born, rather than just "Italy." If your immigrant ancestor married in the United States, the marriage record may provide the birthplaces of the spouses.

Civil birth, marriage and death records vary from state to state, and from one era to another, so it is impossible to know what facts they will add to your family history until you obtain and examine them. They could turn out to be the bridge to your ancestral town in Italy.

One example of a civil birth record is illustrated on page 83. Giuseppe Capellacci was born October 28, 1911, in his family's residence at 421 West 26th Street, New York City. The record names both parents, their respective ages, and the maiden name of the mother (DeFelice). Unfortunately, though, the birthplace of both the father and mother is recorded simply as "Italy"—specifying no *comune* or *provincia* or *regione*.

Visit **www.cdc.gov/nchs/howto/w2w/w2welcom.htm** to learn where to write for vital records. Or check the Internet website of your ancestor's state archives, which normally provides information about obtaining genealogical copies of that state's vital records.

Other State Records. Depending on the state where your ancestors resided, you may find other state-level records that contain facts about their lives. Naturalizations made in state courts, for example, have already been mentioned. Records relating to your forefather's military service if he served in the state guard, or employment records if he worked as a state employee, are also state-level records.

Birth record of Giuseppe Capellacci, born in Manhattan's Little Italy in 1911. Birthplace of both parents is given simply as "Italy"—no region or province or town is specified. However, the document does provide the mother's maiden name, as well as the fact that Giuseppe is her third child, and that all three are living.

To learn what resources exist for the states in which your Italian ancestors lived, consult *Ancestry's Redbook: American State, County & Town Sources* or *Everton's Handybook*. There are also manuals for genealogical research in particular states, and you should visit the Internet website of the state's archives and library too.

If records created and kept on the state level do not yield the information you need to pursue your research in Italian sources, there are still local records to be explored.

Local Records

Records created on the county and town levels—described in *Ancestry's Redbook* and *Everton's Handybook*—are rich in information for Italian-American family history. Here is a sampling of the most important ones.

County Courthouse. County courthouses are teeming with records of potential value for Americans of Italian descent. Real estate deeds, for instance, reveal whether your immigrant ancestor ever purchased land, and if he did, when. The date suggests when the newcomer finally decided to *stay* in America, or at least when he was able financially to buy his own house. (See illustration on p. 85.)

If your ancestor was naturalized in a county court, as discussed above, the record will likely still be found in the county courthouse. Your immigrant ancestor's last will and testament may refer to people and places left behind in Italy; in that case, the probate file will prove most helpful. Lists of voters may indicate when your ancestor became a U.S. citizen. A legal suit brought in circuit court may contain facts about relatives here and abroad. If an ancestor's demise was accidental or suspicious, the coroner's report would explain the circumstances surrounding the incident, perhaps mentioning other family members.

Real estate records may suggest fascinating insight about your ancestors. Italian immigrants in cities tended to rent their lodgings, usually tenement apartments. The purchase of a house reveals two things: 1) the immigrant could afford it; and 2) he had decided to remain in the United States. This 1945 photograph shows Italian-born Francis Carfora (right) standing with family members on the front porch of his Bronx, New York, rowhouse, which he has festooned with American flags to display his patriotism. His son, Joseph, a U.S. Army infantryman, had been captured by the Germans in France, but would soon be welcomed back to the home of this grateful family. (*Photo courtesy of Stephen J. Carfora.*)

For the fullest possible account of the lives of your Italian ancestors on *this* side of the Atlantic, do not neglect to explore thoroughly the records found in the county courthouse.

Cemetery Records and Inscriptions. The record of your immigrant ancestor's burial may reveal the original spelling of his or her surname, date of birth, even native town in Italy. Such records are usually found in the cemetery office, although older ones may have been removed to a local historical society, library or archives. Similar information may be included in the coroner's records in the city or county where your immigrant ancestor died.

Inscriptions on your ancestor's tombstone may include not only his or her name, but also dates of birth and death, and native town as well. Furthermore, artwork on the tombstone is sometimes instructive: the decoration may contain symbols representing your ancestor's religion, occupation, fraternal affiliation in the United States, military involvement or place of origin. In Italy traditional symbols identified the craft or trade of the deceased; these varied from one area of Italy to another. Italian-American sculptors sometimes carried these over into their work for Italian-American families here in the United States, thereby revealing more about a deceased person on his or her tombstone than would appear evident at first sight.

Also quite common on the tombstones of late nineteenth- and early twentieth-century burials—at least in cemeteries in Texas and Louisiana, if not elsewhere—are photographs of the deceased. This, too, was a tradition brought to America by Italian immigrants (more about this under "Italian Cemeteries" in Chapter 7).

If your ancestor worked as a craftsman and belonged to a *società* (trade guild), he may be buried in a "society vault." These mausoleums were built in cemeteries in some states, especially Louisiana—Lake Lawn Metairie Cemetery in New Orleans is the preeminent example (see illustration on p. 88)—by the members of the *società*, who paid a modest monthly amount to ensure a decent burial for themselves and their families. Such vaults are generally surmounted by a statue of the craft's patron saint, and decorated with sculpture and engravings representative of the trade. Members were often from the same town or village in Italy, and this is reflected in the identity of the patron saint and the decoration.

Religious Records. When our Italian ancestors came to the United States, they joined churches and synagogues. So records created by religious communities—mostly Roman Catholic, but also Protestant and Jewish—constitute another source of information about them.

The sacramental registers of parishes in Italian neighborhoods may be especially valuable because the priests who created them retained something of the traditions of their homeland. This means that the baptismal, confirmation, marriage and burial records of Italian parishes tend to contain more information about the people involved than do those of non-Italian parishes.

For instance, the confirmation record of an Italian parishioner and his or her marriage record often include the name of the parish in Italy where the person was baptized, and sometimes even the facts of the baptismal record as well. The relationship of sponsors or witnesses to the principals of the sacred event (brother-in-law, for example, or aunt or cousin) may also be specified—as it is in Italian church registers (more about this in Chapter 5).

Other Local Records. Other types of records created locally—such as city censuses (there is an 1892 Police Census of New York City by neighborhood), naturalizations made in municipal courts, and funeral home records—may

Italian society vaults in Lake Lawn Metairie Cemetery, New Orleans.
(*Photographs by the author.*)

also prove helpful in finding the facts you must know about your immigrant ancestors before turning to Italian records. What you are able to come up with depends on where your ancestors lived and how they participated in the work and social life of their community.

Many of the local resources discussed here, or microfilm copies of them, are held in state archives, libraries and historical societies. But it is always profitable to visit the local library and historical society too, because in the community where your ancestors resided, you are likely to find materials that you will find nowhere else.

Libraries and historical societies usually have an alphabetical name index to obituaries that have appeared in the local newspapers, as well as file cabinets full of newspaper clippings and manuscript and typescript materials pertaining to families of the immediate vicinity. The books and papers of a local Italian-American organization or club, and maybe a collection of the local Italian-language newspaper, would likely be found there too. A visit to the place your Italian ancestors selected for their American home may yield more information about them than you ever thought existed.

Now, having exploited the resources available here in the United States—federal, state and local—you are thoroughly prepared to pursue your family research in the records of Italy. So on now to *la patria!*

4. Civil Records of Italy

However you conduct your research in the historical records of Italy—in person or through correspondence, microfilm, the Internet or a hired assistant—you must familiarize yourself with that country's archives. Most likely, you will eventually be using both civil and religious archives. Civil archives are described in this chapter, religious archives in the next.

The basic administrative configuration of modern Italy has already been explained in Chapter 1. To recapitulate, Italy is divided into twenty *regioni*, which are divided into 103 *provincie*, which encompass hundreds of *comuni* and *frazioni di comune* (see map of contemporary Italy on pp. 92–93). Comparing Italy to the United States, you might think of *regioni* as states, *provincie* as counties, *comuni* as townships and *frazioni* as unincorporated hamlets.

This rough parallel, however, does not apply to Italy's archival system. In the United States state archives are vital to genealogical research, but in Italy there are *no* record repositories on the regional level. It is on the *provincial* level that you find the principal archives for Italian genealogy. In almost every *capo luogo* (94 out of the 103), there is an *archivio di stato* (state archives; plural is *archivi di stato*). Some *archivi di stato* with particularly large collections have a *sezione* (department or branch) in one or two lesser cities of the province too.

There is also the *Archivio Centrale dello Stato* (Central State Archives) in Rome, but here again the comparison

Contemporary Italy. (*Drawn by the author.*)

CONTEMPORARY ITALY

*(Each province is listed with its abbreviation and
the first two digits of its five-digit postal code)*

I. ABRUZZO
1. Chieti (CH, 66)
2. L'Aquila (AQ, 67)
3. Pescara (PE, 65)
4. Teramo (TE, 64)

II. BASILICATA
5. Matera (MT, 75)
6. Potenza (PZ, 85)

III. CALABRIA
7. Catanzaro (CZ, 88)
8. Cosenza (CS, 87)
9. Crotone (KR, 88)
10. Reggio Calabria (RC, 89)
11. Vibo Valentia (VV, 88)

IV. CAMPANIA
12. Avellino (AV, 83)
13. Benevento (BN, 82)
14. Caserta (CE, 81)
15. Napoli = Naples (NA, 80)
16. Salerno (SA, 84)

V. EMILIA-ROMAGNA
17. Bologna (BO, 40)
18. Ferrara (FE, 44)
19. Forli (FO, 47)
20. Modena (MO, 41)
21. Parma (PR, 43)
22. Piacenza (PC, 29)
23. Ravenna (RA, 48)
24. Reggio Emilia (RE, 42)
25. Rimini (RN, 47)

VI. FRIULI-VENEZIA GIULIA
26. Gorizia (GO, 34)
27. Pordenone (PN, 33)
28. Trieste (TS, 34)
29. Udine (UD, 33)

VII. LAZIO = LATIUM
30. Frosinone (FR, 03)
31. Latina (LT, 04)
32. Rieti (RI, 02)
33. Roma = Rome (ROMA, 00)
34. Viterbo (VT, 01)

VIII. LIGURIA
35. Genova = Genoa (GE, 16)
36. Imperia (IM, 18)
37. La Spezia (SP, 19)
38. Savona (SV, 17)

IX. LOMBARDIA = LOMBARDY
39. Bergamo (BG, 24)
40. Brescia (BS, 25)
41. Como (CO, 22)
42. Cremona (CR, 26)
43. Lecco (LC, 22)
44. Lodi (LO, 20)
45. Mantova (MN, 46)
46. Milano = Milan (MI, 20)
47. Pavia (PV, 27)
48. Sondrio (SO, 23)
49. Varese (VA, 21)

X. MARCHE
50. Ancona (AN, 60)
51. Ascoli Piceno (AP, 63)
52. Macerata (MC, 62)
53. Pesaro-Urbino (PS, 61)

XI. MOLISE
54. Campobasso (CB, 86)
55. Isernia (IS, 86)

XII. PIEMONTE = PIEDMONT
56. Alessandria (AL, 15)
57. Asti (AT, 14)
58. Biella (BI, 13)
59. Cuneo (CN, 12)
60. Novara (NO, 28)
61. Torino = Turin (TO, 10)
62. Verbano-Cusio-Ossola (VB, 28)
63. Vercelli (VC, 13)

XIII. PUGLIA = APULIA
64. Bari (BA, 70)
65. Brindisi (BR, 72)
66. Foggia (FG, 71)
67. Lecce (LE, 73)
68. Taranto (TA, 74)

XIV. SARDEGNA = SARDINIA
69. Cagliari (CA, 09)
70. Nuoro (NU, 08)
71. Oristano (OR, 09)
72. Sassari (SS, 07)

XV. SICILIA = SICILY
73. Agrigento (AG, 92)
74. Caltanissetta (CL, 93)
75. Catania (CT, 95)
76. Enna (EN, 94)
77. Messina (ME, 98)
78. Palermo (PA, 90)
79. Ragusa (RG, 97)
80. Siracusa (SR, 96)
81. Trapani (TP, 91)

XVI. TOSCANA = TUSCANY
82. Arezzo (AR, 52)
83. Firenze = Florence (FI, 50)
84. Grosseto (GR, 58)
85. Livorno = Leghorn (LI, 57)
86. Lucca (LU, 55)
87. Massa Carrara (MS, 54)
88. Pisa (PI, 56)
89. Pistoia (PT, 51)
90. Prato (PO, 50)
91. Siena (SI, 53)

XVII. TRENTINO-ALTO ADIGE
92. Bolzano (BZ, 39)
93. Trento (TN, 38)

XVIII. UMBRIA
94. Perugia (PG, 06)
95. Terni (TR, 05)

XIX. VALLE D'AOSTA
96. Aosta (AO, 11)

XX. VENETO
97. Belluno (BL, 32)
98. Padova = Padua (PD, 35)
99. Rovigo (RO, 45)
100. Treviso (TV, 31)
101. Venezia = Venice (VE, 30)
102. Verona (VR, 37)
103. Vicenza (VI, 36)

with the United States falls short. Whereas the National Archives in Washington, D.C., is a repository of primary importance for American genealogy, as Chapter 3 has shown, the *Archivio Centrale dello Stato* in Rome, which will be described below, contains no records of use to most family historians.

Archivi di stato are the principal repositories for Italian genealogy insofar as they hold Italy's vast treasure of pre-1870 public records. The Church of Jesus Christ of Latter-day Saints has microfilmed millions of Italian records of genealogical value in the *archivi di stato*. But *archivi di stato* are certainly not the only repositories useful to family historians. If the U.S. sources described in Chapters 1, 2 and 3 do not provide sufficient information about your forebears for you to delve into Italy's pre-1870 records in *archivi di stato*, you will need to begin your search on the local level, in the *archivio comunale* (town archives) of the community where your ancestors lived. There you will find more recent records.

Every *comune* has its *municipio* (town hall), and in every *municipio* is the archives of public records pertaining to its citizens. But these *archivi comunali* (sometimes called *archivi municipali*) have not been microfilmed by the LDS church for its Family History Library. That is why it is often in the *municipio* of your immigrant ancestor's native *comune* that your family research in Italy begins. Only after you have established the branches of your family tree back to 1870 can you turn to the records in the *archivi di stato*. For this reason the major records in the *archivio comunale* will be described first, and those in the *archivio di stato* afterward.

First of all, however, it is important to note that the civil records described below vary widely in the amount and type of information they contain, in the accuracy of that information, and in their physical condition. Italy as a modern nation is young; it was unified from numerous independent states during the 1860s, and only became a single country with its capital at Rome in 1870.

Trafford R. Cole, an American who has lived in Italy and worked as a professional genealogist for many years, authored a series of four articles in *POINTers* in 1991–92 (reprinted in 2001–02) detailing numerous regional distinctions among Italian record sources. He concluded his sketch of Italian history this way: "Thus, at the end of the 1700s, one finds Italy divided into a series of city states and principalities in the north, with a tradition of Austrian influence; the Papal states in the center; and two Spanish kingdoms in the south, one of Naples and the other of Sicily; all with very different customs, traditions and language." (See map of pre-unification Italy on pp. 96–97.)

Each of these sovereign states experienced wars and natural disasters and changes in leadership and administration, and each kept its records in its own way. "Just to give an example," Trafford Cole wrote, "a common name Giovanni (John) in most early documents will appear in the Latin form of Joannes or Johannes, but in the Venetian area, it will be written in the dialect form of Zuanne." Naturally, therefore, no record description could possibly be universally true throughout the whole of Italy.

It was Napoleon Bonaparte who, during his brief reign as King of Italy from 1806 to 1815, unified the administrative, judicial and legislative system of the entire country into one substantially similar to the one described above. (Napoleone Buonaparte, who later gallicized his name to Napoleon Bonaparte, was born of Italian parentage in Ajaccio, Corsica, in 1769. Corsica had been acquired from Italy by France just two years earlier.) Though Italy was restored to its pre-Napoleonic autonomous states by the Congress of Vienna in 1815, the Emperor's system of *regioni, provincie, comuni* and *frazioni* remained the model for modern-day Italy.

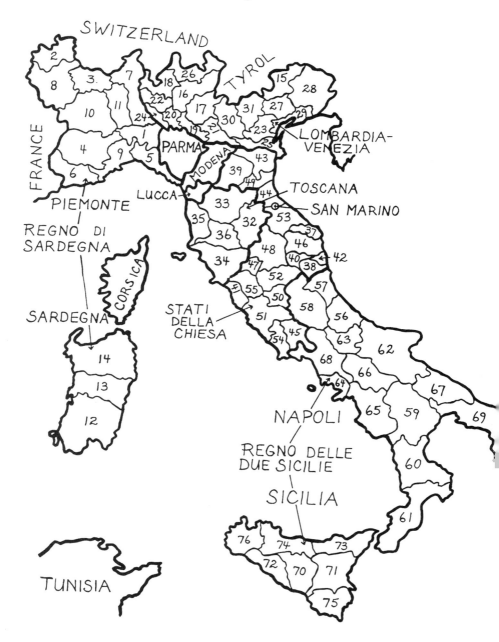

Pre-Unification Italy. *(Drawn by the author.)*

PRE-UNIFICATION ITALY (1859)

REGNO DI SARDEGNA =
KINGDOM OF SARDINIA

PIEMONTE = PIEDMONT
1. Alessandria
2. Anneci
3. Aosta
4. Coni
5. Genova
6. Nizza
7. Novara
8. Savoia
9. Savona
10. Torino
11. Vercelli

SARDEGNA = SARDINIA
12. Cagliari
13. Nuoro
14. Sassari

LOMBARDIA-VENEZIA =
LOMBARDY-VENICE
15. Belluno
16. Bergamo
17. Brescia
18. Como
19. Cremona
20. Lodi
21. Mantova
22. Milano
23. Padova
24. Pavia
25. Polesina
26. Sondrio
27. Treviso
28. Udine
29. Venezia
30. Verona
31. Vicenza

PARMA

MODENA

LUCCA

TOSCANA = TUSCANY
32. Arezzo
33. Firenze
34. Grossetto
35. Pisa
36. Siena

STATI DELLA CHIESA =
PAPAL STATES
37. Ancona
38. Ascoli
39. Bologna
40. Camerino
41. Civita Vecchia
42. Fermo
43. Ferrara
44. Forli
45. Frosinone
46. Macerata
47. Orvieto
48. Perugia
49. Ravenna
50. Rieti
51. Roma
52. Spoleto
53. Urbino & Pesaro
54. Velletri
55. Viterbo

REGNO DELLE DUE SICILIE =
KINGDOM OF THE TWO SICILIES

NAPOLI = NAPLES
56. Abbruzzo Citra
57. Abbruzzo Ultra 1
58. Abbruzzo Ultra 2
59. Basilicata
60. Calabria Citra
61. Calabria Ultra
62. Capitanata
63. Molise
64. Napoli
65. Principato Citra
66. Principato Ultra
67. Terra di Bari
68. Terra di Lavoro
69. Terra d'Otranto

SICILIA = SICILY
70. Caltanisetta
71. Catania
72. Girgenti
73. Messina
74. Palermo
75. Siragosa
76. Trapani

By 1860 King Vittorio Emanuele II of Piedmont had emerged as the champion of Italian unification. Between 1860 and 1865 Garibaldi and his Redshirts, devoted subjects of Vittorio Emanuele, captured Sicily and Naples for their king. In 1866, as a result of war with Austria, the king also gained Venice as part of his realm. Finally, by treaty with the Pope in 1870, Italy as a united country, with Rome as its capital city, was born. (For more information about the history and formation of Italy, see the "General Histories of Italy" section of the Bibliography.)

The following descriptions of Italian civil records, therefore, are helpful generalizations. You will discover soon enough in your own search for Italian ancestors just how much these descriptions may vary from the norm in any particular locality and era.

Archivio Comunale (Town Archives)

According to Italian law, the registers comprising the *archivio comunale* may only be searched by an official working in the *municipio*. (Another term for *municipio* is *casa comunale*.) Just how much searching and reporting such an official will perform for an American—who either writes or shows up in person—varies widely not only from one *comune* to another, but from one clerk to another in the same *municipio*. Some are more cooperative and helpful than others.

On occasion, an American who speaks directly to the clerk's superior—the *ufficiale dello stato civile* (official in charge of vital records) or the *direttore* (director)—may be allowed to search through the registers himself, one at a time. But this happy scenario is very rare. The more specific and accurate the information you provide, the better the chances you will receive a positive reaction from the clerk. It is good to keep in mind that a town hall is a functioning public office and is neither intended nor staffed to render assistance to historical researchers.

In all of your dealings with the civil servants in your ancestral towns, be mindful to put your best foot forward, show due respect, smile, cooperate, and be patient and considerate and as helpful as you can possibly be. Remember, it is *their* country; *you* are the outsider making requests of them. It is both appropriate and expected that you acquiesce to their way of doing things. Express your appreciation; say *"Grazie tante!"* ("Many thanks!") many times. To the Italians you meet, in person or in writing, you represent Americans, and your demeanor influences their impression of the United States as a whole.

There are no published guidebooks to these *archivi comunali*. They differ vastly from one town to the next. However, one reference work that includes practical information is the *Guida Monaci: Annuario Generale Italiano* (*Monaci Guide: General Italian Annual*). This weighty tome, updated every year, is a directory of all of Italy's governmental offices and agencies. It lists every public archives and library in the country, with their address, phone number and director's name. In addition, websites of individual *comuni* (discussed under "Maps and Gazetteers," p. 49) are very helpful.

Stato Civile. Birth, marriage and death records, called *stato civile* (vital records), have been kept uniformly throughout Italy since 1870. (Earlier *stato civile* for some *regioni* will be discussed under "Archivio di Stato" below.) They are maintained by the *ufficio di stato civile* (office of vital records) in the *municipio* and are rich in family information.

Atto di Nascita. To create an *atto di nascita* (birth record), the infant—normally less than one day old—had to be presented physically to the town's *ufficiale dello stato civile*. The official in charge of vital records was usually the *sindaco* (mayor), who would be found in the *municipio* or *casa comunale*. The presenter was usually the father, but sometimes another male relative or the midwife.

The record contains the date of the presentation; name, age, profession and place of residence of the presenter; maiden name, age and place of residence of the mother; name, age, profession and place of residence of the father; date, hour and place of birth of the infant, and his or her name; and the names, ages, professions and places of residence of two witnesses to the presentation. In many localities of Italy this information is written on the left side of the page, and on the right side is a brief record of the infant's baptism—usually occurring the same day or the next—which gives the date and parish of the baptism.

The *atto di nascita* on p. 102 records the birth of Rosa Fascella on 21 October 1829 in the Sicilian *comune* of Misilmeri. The *atto* was penned at 3 P.M., when the proud father, Gaetano Fascella, carried his new *fanciulla* (baby girl) into the *casa comunale*. He told the *ufficiale* (who happened to be the mayor of the town, the *sindaco*) that she had been born that morning in his house at 11 A.M., making the infant just four hours old when her debut into the world was recorded for all time.

Note that the record volumes were printed with blank spaces where the *ufficiale dello stato civile* wrote in the particular facts of each birth. Note, too, that most numbers, including dates, were spelled out in words, rather than using numerals. Mayor Gallecci's penmanship is typical of the period, and about as legible as you will find in old Italian records. (In the spring 1994 issue of *POINTers* [vol. 8, no. 1], an article by Francis J. Arduini was illustrated with excerpts from *stato civile* showing a vast array of handwritings.)

A child whose parents are recorded as *padre ignoto* (father unknown) and *madre ignota* (mother unknown) was usually a foundling. On occasion, the father and mother of a newborn whose parentage was unknown might simply be recorded as *proietto* (derived from the fact, perhaps, that the infant has been "cast out" or "cast aside" by them). In such cases the presenter is often a woman.

Many Italian villages used to have an elderly woman, unmarried, a widow perhaps, who acted as the acknowledged "orphan lady." Unwanted babies, generally illegitimate, could be left on her doorstep with the assurance that they would be cared for. If you scan the birth registers of any particular town, you will see this same woman's name reappear from time to time over the years. Obviously, unless some tradition about the birth has been passed on orally within the family, tracing the parentage of such a foundling may be impossible.

A child whose mother's name is recorded, but whose father is given as *padre ignoto* or *padre incerto* (father uncertain), was often a child born out of wedlock. Here again, discovering the father's name and tracing the child's paternal ancestry may be impossible. The name of the presenter, however, and the names of the witnesses may provide clues that, in conjunction with exhaustive research on all members of the extended family, allow you to hypothesize who the father possibly was.

In the poor rural culture of pre-industrial Italy, children born out of wedlock were often simply "taken in" by the mother's family—*some* branch of the mother's family—without any legal formalities or paperwork whatsoever. The "adoptee" would assume the family's surname and be raised along with all the other children as just another member of the family. In the absence of any orally transmitted explanation, the full human story and the surname of the father will probably remain mysteries forever.

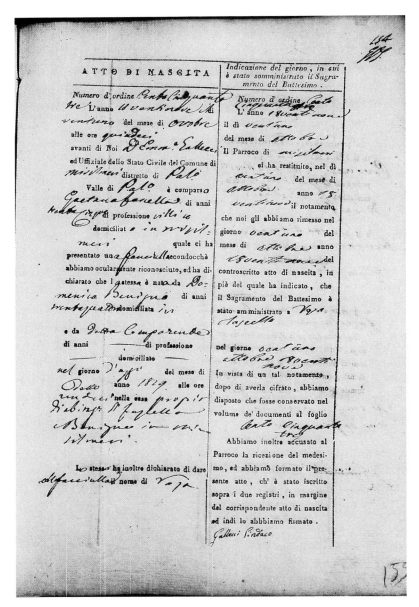

First page of a typical 2-page *atto di nascita*, recording the birth of Rosa Fascella, daughter of Gaetano Fascella and Domenica Benigno, on 21 October 1829 in the *comune* of Misilmeri, *provincia* of Palermo. (*Photograph courtesy of the Latter-day Saints Family History Library.*)

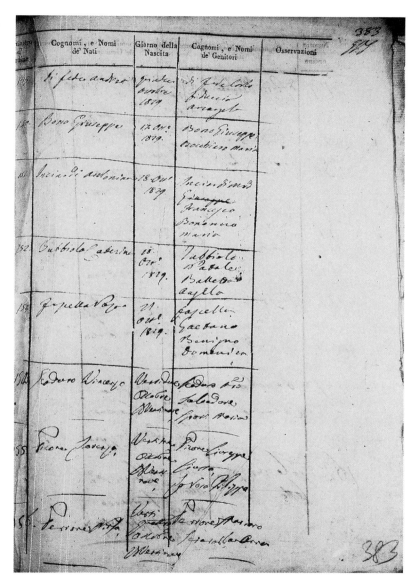

Page from a typical index found at the end of a register of births, showing that the record of "Fascella Rosa," born 21 October 1829, of Fascella Gaetano and Benigno Domenica is record number 153 in the register. (*Photograph courtesy of the Latter-day Saints Family History Library.*)

Sometimes, when a person married or died in a *comune* other than his or her native *comune*, the *ufficiale dello stato civile* recording the event would forward the information to the *ufficiale dello stato civile* in the *comune* of birth, who in turn would annotate the original *atto di nascita*. This practice has been observed with varying regularity across the country and across the years.

When an infant was too weak to be carried to the town hall on the day of its birth, or entered the world in the middle of the night, the father might make the presentation a day or two later. If the presenter did not make it clear that the new life was already a day or two old, from force of habit the *ufficiale* would simply insert that the infant was born *"lo stesso"* ("the same day"). Many an Italian ancestor was born before the birth date penned into the civil register. My grandmother Colletta, for instance, maintained steadfastly, based on what her mother had told her, that she was born two days prior to her "official" birthday.

Atto della Solenne Promessa di Celebrare il Matrimonio. A marriage record is called an *atto della solenne promessa di celebrare il matrimonio* (record of the solemn promise to celebrate matrimony) because the marriage itself was not contracted at city hall, but rather in the religious ceremony that followed in the church. To create an *atto della solenne promessa*, the bride and groom would appear before the *ufficiale dello stato civile* with four witnesses.

The record contains the date of the appearance; name, age, birthplace, profession and place of residence of the groom; his father's name, age, profession and place of residence; his mother's maiden name, age and place of residence; name, age, birthplace and place of residence of the bride; her father's name, age, profession and place of residence; her mother's maiden name, age and place of residence; and the names, ages, professions and places of residence of the four witnesses.

If the groom is a widower, or the bride a widow, this will be stated also, sometimes with the name of the former spouse. Occasionally the date and place of death of that former spouse will also be indicated. Those principals who could write signed their names at the end of the record. In many localities of Italy this information is written on the left side of the page, and the right side contains a brief record of the sacramental union that followed in the church.

The *atto della solenne promessa* on p. 106 records the betrothal and subsequent marriage of Don Leopoldo Girgenti and Donna Giuseppa LoMonaco in Bagheria, Sicily, on 10 October 1824. Notice the titles of the groom and bride, *Don* (lord) and *Donna* (lady). In a society as rigidly divided into classes as Italy has traditionally been over the centuries, you are liable to come across titles in the records of your ancestors. Be aware that the use of titles varied in meaning from one place to another and from one time to another.

For example, Donna Giuseppa LoMonaco, the bride, is the daughter of "*Maestro* Cosimo." *Maestro*, meaning "Master" (*Magister* in Latin), is often found in old Italian records before the name of a craftsman. This term of respect indicates that the craftsman had achieved a level of mastery that entitled him to take on apprentices—and use the title. Cosimo LoMonaco is clearly a master *bottaio* (cooper; maker of wooden casks and tubs).

However, *Don* before a man's name and *Donna* before a woman's name may or may not indicate noble birth. Sometimes they simply served as titles of respect and deference for a person of prominence in the community—someone with great wealth, education or political position. All of these in historical Italy translated into someone with *power*, which may have been achieved and retained *not* through noble lineage, but rather through personal ambition and self-improvement somewhere back in the family tree.

First page of a typical 4-page *atto della solenne promessa*, recording the marriage of Don Leopoldo Girgenti and Donna Giuseppa LoMonaco on 10 October 1824 in the *comune* of Bagheria, *provincia* of Palermo. (*Photograph courtesy of the Latter-day Saints Family History Library.*)

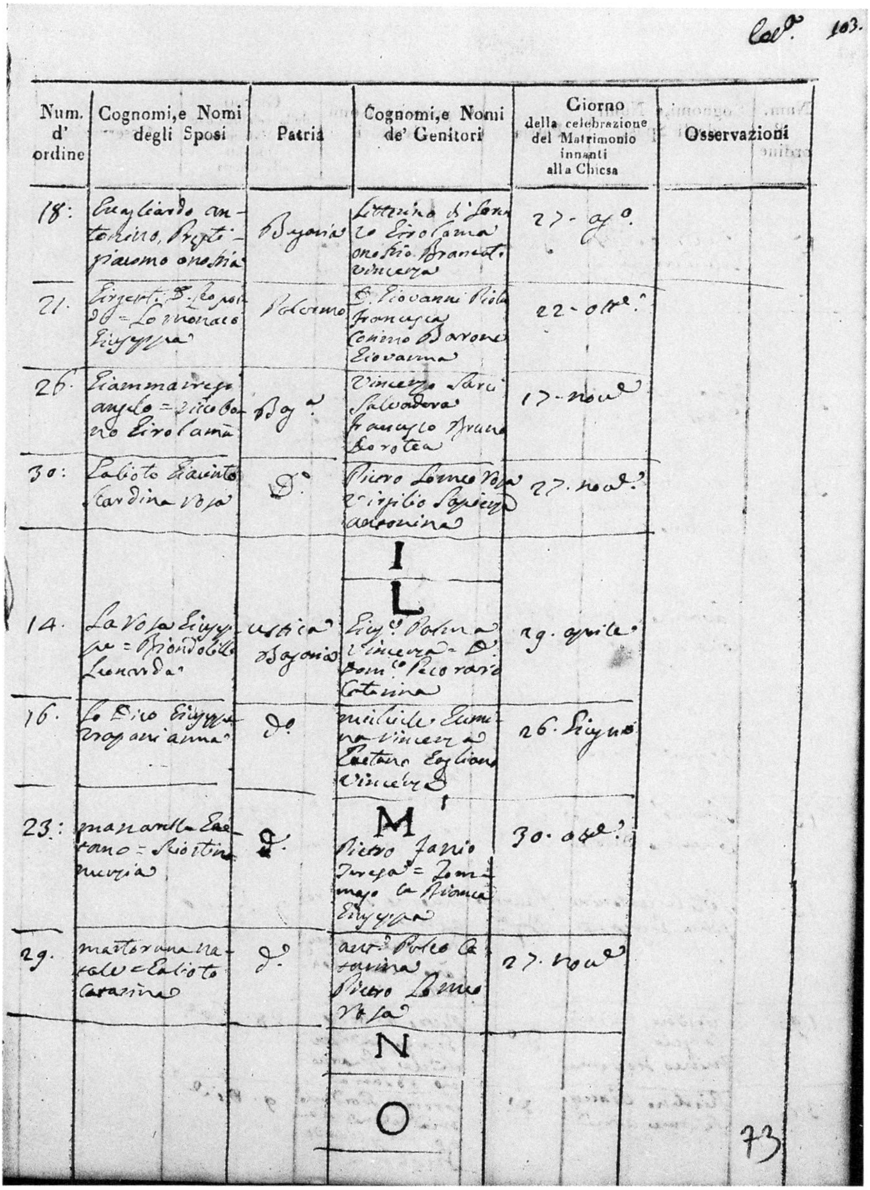

Col° 103.

Num. d' ordine	Cognomi,e Nomi degli Sposi	Patria	Cognomi,e Nomi de' Genitori	Giorno della celebrazione del Matrimonio innanti alla Chicsa	Osservazioni
18	*[handwritten]*	*[handwritten]*	*[handwritten]*	27 - ag°	
21	*[handwritten]*	*[handwritten]*	*[handwritten]*	22 - ott.	
26	*[handwritten]*	*[handwritten]*	*[handwritten]*	17 - nov	
30	*[handwritten]*	*[handwritten]*	*[handwritten]*	27 - nod.	

I

L

14	*[handwritten]*	*[handwritten]*	*[handwritten]*	29. aprile	
16	*[handwritten]*	*[handwritten]*	*[handwritten]*	26. giugno	
23	*[handwritten]*	*[handwritten]*	*[handwritten]*	30. ott.	
29	*[handwritten]*	*[handwritten]*	*[handwritten]*	27 - nov	

M

N

O

Page from a typical index found at the end of a register of marriages, showing that the record for "Girgenti, D. Leopoldo = LoMonaco, D. Giuseppa" is record number 21 in the register. (*Photograph courtesy of the Latter-day Saints Family History Library.*)

Often *Don* and *Donna* were used for persons whose families were of noble origin, with the attendant wealth and power, but long since reduced in circumstances. As already remarked in "Genealogies of Titled Families" above, "downward mobility" occurred often and everywhere, for a variety of reasons, throughout Italy's privileged classes.

The groom's father, Don Giovanni Girgenti, is a *trafficante* (merchant) of the city of Palermo, and ostensibly a prosperous one. This social status alone could account for the use of the title *Don*, although his son, the groom, also called *Don*, is only a modest *caffettiere* (café owner). Nevertheless, he is marrying the daughter of a master cooper.

Although the bride and groom's fathers are still living on this wedding day in 1824, their mothers are both deceased. This is obvious from the use of the word *fu* before the mothers' names. Literally, *fu* means "was." In Italian records it indicates a deceased person. When the parent of an individual named in a record is still living at the time the record is created, the relationship is indicated using *di*. For example, "Leopoldo Girgenti, figlio *di* Giovanni" means "Leopoldo Girgenti, son of Giovanni, *who is living*." However, when the parent is deceased at the time the record is created, the relationship is indicated using *del fu* for the father and *della fu* for the mother. For example, "Giuseppa LoMonaco, figlia *della fu* Giovanna Barrocca" means "Giuseppa LoMonaco, daughter of the *deceased* Giovanna Barrocca."

But frequently, for expedience, the *del* or *della* was dropped, and the word *fu* alone was used in place of the word *di* to indicate a deceased parent; for example, "Concetta, figlia fu Antonio." This practice may help you find an ancestor's date of death. For example, if an 1842 marriage record indicates the mother of the bride Paolina as "di Maria," and the 1844 marriage record of Paolina's sister Anna gives her mother as "fu Maria," it is evident that Maria died sometime between the marriage dates of her two daughters in 1842 and 1844.

When searching for your ancestors' marriage records, remember that in Italy weddings customarily took place in the bride's parish, not the groom's.

Atto di Morto. An *atto di morto* (death record) is as rich in personal information as an *atto di nascita* and an *atto della solenne promessa*. Besides stating the name and age of the deceased, and his or her date and place of death, it usually gives the deceased person's occupation, place of residence and names of parents and spouse, if the deceased was married. If the deceased was a widow or widower, the name of the last spouse is given. An *atto di morto* may also contain the name of the individual who came to the *casa comunale* to report the death to the *ufficiale dello stato civile*. A married woman or widow will appear in the death record under her maiden name, not her husband's name.

The *stato civile* just described are usually kept in volumes by year, and most volumes are indexed alphabetically by surname in the back (see illustrations on pp. 103 and 107). Indexes arranged alphabetically by given name rather than surname are also known to exist. Some *stato civile* also have ten-year cumulative indexes, called *indici decennali*, which normally encompass a complete decade each, such as 1870–80, 1880–90, 1890–1900, and so forth.

It has already been stated that a great deal of Italy's *stato civile* has been microfilmed by The Church of Jesus Christ of Latter-day Saints and is graciously made available to the general public. But that happy news bears repeating. Today, using your local Family History Center, you may accomplish extensive research in Italian records without ever leaving your own community. Thirty years ago that was simply not possible.

Instructions on how to secure information from *stato civile* by corresponding with the Italian repositories holding the old volumes will be discussed in Chapter 7. If you do choose to write to your ancestors' *comuni*, you may request two other types of family records. These are *not* original historical records, but rather documents prepared specifically for you from original historical records in the *archivio municipale*. They are the *certificato di stato di famiglia* and the *certificato de residenza*.

Certificato di Stato di Famiglia. A *certificato di stato di famiglia* (certificate of family status), sometimes called a *certificato di situazione di famiglia*, is a table of lines and columns that is filled in with statistical information about a single household. A household includes all of the relatives residing together as a family—parents, children, grandchildren, in-laws and others, even those family members who are deceased when the *certificato* is created.

The *certificato* bears each person's name, relationship to the head of the household, birth date, birthplace and, in the column headed *Annotazioni* (Annotations), information about his or her marriage, death date, occupation or date of emigration (sometimes the destination too). Occasionally even the names of the parents of the head of household and his wife—which is to say, another generation of the family—are indicated. A *certificato di stato di famiglia* is a genealogical "spreadsheet" of one family unit.

You request a certificate from the *sindaco* or *ufficio dello stato civile* of your ancestors' *comune*, and it is prepared by a member of the *municipio* staff using records kept by the *ufficio di anagrafe* (office of the census). This office has no equivalent in the United States, but resembles the one that used to exist in the town halls of seventeenth- and eighteenth-century New England, where vital records were kept by family unit. The *ufficiale di anagrafe* (census official) compiles information on each of the town's families from a variety of public records found in the *municipio*—vital records, censuses, residency/property ownership records, records of emigration, military service, etc. These are the sources used to complete a *certificato di stato di famiglia*.

Anagrafe records may include *Registri di Popolazione* (Population Registers) that date from the late nineteenth and early twentieth centuries (see illustrations on pp. 113–115). These large folios contain detailed information about every one of the town's families, with changes in status (births, marriages, deaths, emigration, etc.) penned into the record as they occurred. Other *anagrafe* records are the *censimenti* (population censuses), which will be discussed below. Since the first national population census to include the name and vital statistics of every person in every household was not taken until 1911, some *ufficiali di stato civile* may not prepare a *certificato di stato di famiglia* with information pre-dating what is available in the 1911 census.

On the other hand, sometimes an *ufficiale* will compile a *certificato* of a nineteenth-century family by using the town's original *stato civile*. But such an undertaking requires considerable searching through the old birth, marriage and death registers, and many *municipi* simply do not have sufficient staff to offer this service. When they do, it is a potentially expensive proposition for the requester, and the document's completeness and reliability depend on the ability and conscientiousness of the preparer.

Of course, if the Family History Library has the *stato civile* of your ancestral *comune* on microfilm, you may prepare a *certificato* yourself by doing your own searching in the filmed records.

The *situazione di stato di famiglia* illustrated on p. 116 was created in 1999 and shows the household of Andrea Montanari, a porter. He, his wife, children, grandchildren and daughter-in-law were all born in the *comune* of San Giovanni in Persiceto, Province of Bologna, in the Region of Emilia-Romagna.

Andrea's eldest son, Enrico, died unmarried at the young age of 17, and his two younger children, Luigi and Giuseppe, both died in infancy. However, his eldest daughter, Adele, married and lived to be 85. She died in the village in which she was born. The second son, Saturno, married in Italy, then immigrated in March 1913 to America, where he was joined by his eldest son in 1914, and finally by his wife and remaining two children in October 1915. By this time Andrea Montanari and his wife had both gone on *a megliore vita* (to a better life).

For comparison, the *certificato di stato di famiglia* illustrated on p. 117 was compiled in 2000 and depicts the household of Carlo Balboni, whose occupation is not given. He and his family resided in his native Renazzo (a *frazione* of the *comune* of Cento), Province of Ferrara, in the Region of Emilia-Romagna. Notice that when the compiler was unable to come up with a death date, he at least noted, "*non censito nel 1921*" ("does not appear in the 1921 census").

This *certificato* implies an intriguing tale. The younger of Carlo's two daughters, Emma, gave birth to a son in 1895 without the benefit of marriage. The boy's paternity is given as "N.N.," meaning "*non notato*," ("not recorded"). The following year Emma moved to the neighboring town of Bondeno, presumably with her baby. It is up to the family historian to discover whether the ending to Emma's story is happy or sad.

Notice that Italian officials always put the family name first, in capital letters, followed by the given name, when excerpting information from old records. Writing names this way in official documents is standard procedure in Italy (for another example, see the notarial deed pictured on p. 127).

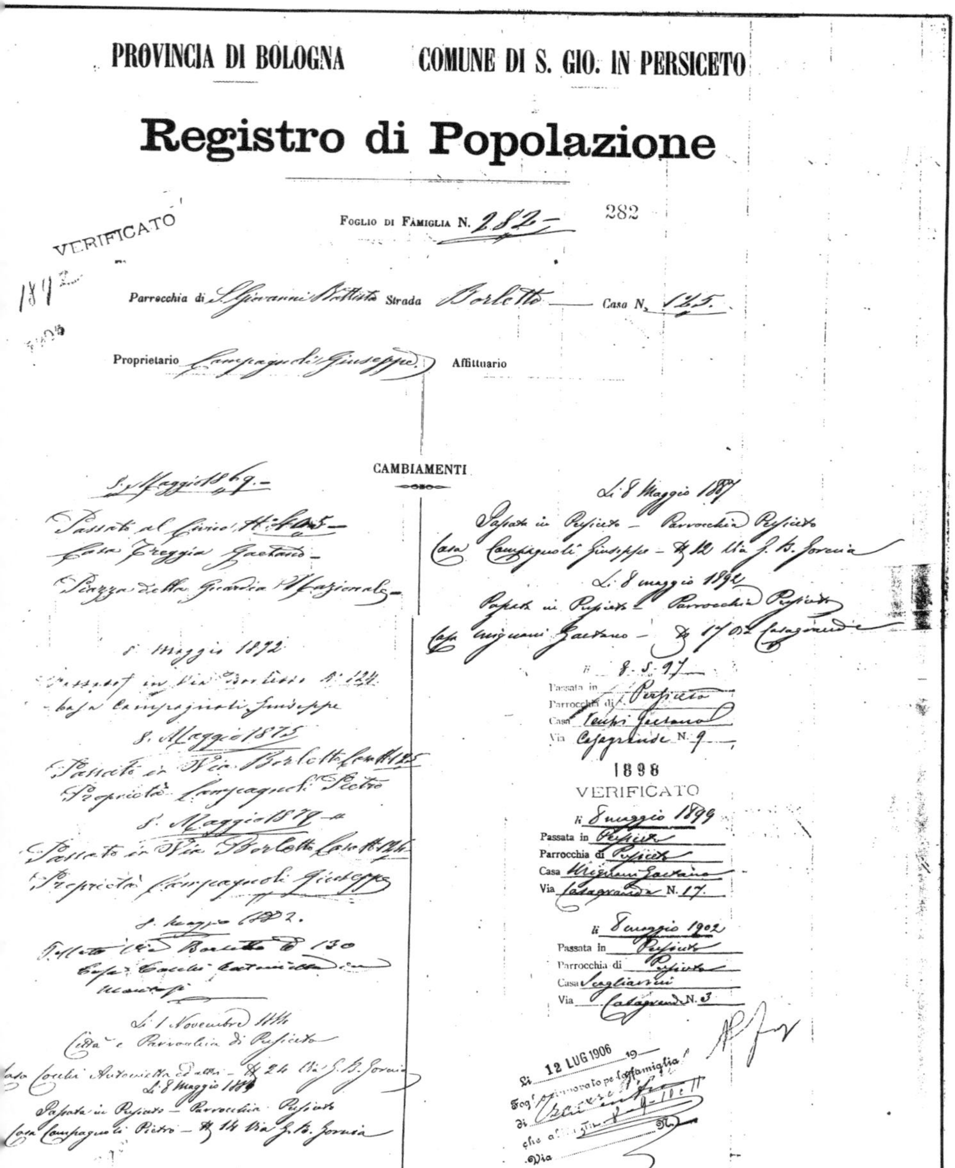

PROVINCIA DI BOLOGNA **COMUNE DI S. GIO. IN PERSICETO**

Registro di Popolazione

VERIFICATO

Foglio di Famiglia N. *282* — 282

Parrocchia di *S. Giovanni Battista* Strada *Borletto* — Casa N. *145*

Proprietario *Campagnoli Giuseppe* Affittuario

CAMBIAMENTI

(handwritten entries documenting family address changes, largely illegible)

1898
VERIFICATO

Three pages from the *Registro di Popolazione* for the *comune* of San Giovanni in Persiceto, *Provincia* of Bologna, *Regione* of Emilio-Romagna, detailing the family of Andrea Montanari. The first page, under *Cambiamenti* (Changes), shows that the family rented houses at several different addresses between 1869 and 1906. *(Continued)*

282

N.º d'ordine delle persone componenti la famiglia	COGNOME	NOME	PATERNITÀ	MATERNITÀ	SESSO		Relazione di parentela o di convivenza col Capo della Famiglia	Professione, Condizione, Mestiere	Luogo della Nascita	Data della Nascita	STATO CIVILE		
					Maschi	Femmine					Celibi	Coniugati	Vedovi
1	Montana	Andrea	fu Antonio	fu Messieri Esa	M		Capo della Famiglia	Facchino	Persiceto Venezzano	1838		Marito di Montana Matilde	
2	Andorlini	Matilde	fu Giuseppe	fu Trerzoni Lucia		F	Moglie	Donna	Persiceto Mart...	1839		Moglie di Montana Andrea	
3	Montanari	Enrico	Andrea	Andorlini Matilde	M		Figlio	Persiceto	1864		C		
4	Montanari	Adele	"	"		F	Figlia			1868		C	
5	Montanari	Saturno	"	"	M		Figlio	falegname	"	1870		C	
6	Montanari	Luigi	"	"	M		"		"	1872		C	
7	Montanari	Giuseppe	"	"	M		"		"	1873		C	
8	Vecchi	Virginia	Carlo	Collina Virginia		F	nuora			1868		Moglie di Montana Saturno	
9	Montanari	Alberto	Saturno	Vecchi Virginia	M		Nipote		Persiceto	1892		C	
10	"	Saturno Ferdinando	"	"	M		"		"	1895		C	
11	"	Adele	"	"		F	"		"	1901		C	

Pages two and three provide a wealth of biographical information about Andrea, his wife, six children and three grandchildren, including the following information for each one: surname, name, name of father and mother, and whether that parent is living or deceased, sex, relationship to the head of household, trade or profession, date and place of birth, marital status, legal address and actual residence, changes of address, date

Data dell' ingresso nel Comune	LUOGO			Luogo in cui va a stabilirsi in caso di cambiamento di residenza	DATA		Cambiamenti nello stato civile con indicazione della data	Se sa leggere	Se sa scrivere	ETTARI			OSSERVAZIONI
	del domicilio legale	di residenza od abitazione	dell' ultima residenza		dell' uscita dal Comune	della morte				Boaria o padronale	Mezzadria	Totale	
	Perricto Perricto							ẞ. ẞ.					*8 maggio 1896. N. 1.2. (2gr.* *2. al f. 26. Capres*
	"	"						" "					
	"	"			*1579*			" "					
	"	"					*9. 6ytr. 1889 ẞ. 6.* *9. con Evange nostphorni*						*N. 4. Caffola al f. 340. Luwd*
	"	"					*31 maggio 1892 ẞ. ẞ. coniugato al Vecchi Virginia*						
	"	"			*1172 29 Agosto*								
	"	"			*1574 11 Gennaio*								
	"	"						ẞ. ẞ.					*N. 4. Avuto dal f. 128 Bus*
	"	"											
	"	"											
	"	"											

when left the *comune* or died, changes in marital status, with date, whether able to read and write, renter or owner, and special notations. This is the type of record kept in the *ufficio di anagrafe* for all families of the *comune*. (*Photocopied document courtesy of Marcia Iannizzi Melnyk.*)

Certificato N.

COMUNE DI S. GIOVANNI IN PERSICETO

Provincia di Bologna

IL SINDACO

visti gli atti di anagrafe, certifica risultare dagli stessi lo sottoscritto

SITUAZIONE DI FAMIGLIA STORICA – all'origine

al nome di ___MONTANARI ANDREA___ qui residente in Via ___Borletto N. 125 – Parrocchia di S.Giovanni Battista___

N.	COGNOME E NOME	Luogo di nascita	Data di nascita	Stato Civile	Relazione di parentela	ANNOTAZIONI
1	MONTANARI ANDREA di Antonio e Messieri Rosa	S.G.Persiceto Zenerigolo	9.11.1827	cg.	I.S.	deceduto a S.G.Persiceto il 12.8.1908
2	ANDERLINI MATILDE di Giuseppe e Guerzoni Lucia	S.G.Persiceto Martignone	27.6.1832	Moglie	deceduta a S.G.Persiceto il 29.11.1912
3	MONTANARI ENRICO di Andrea e Anderlini Matilde	S.G.Persiceto	2.6.1861	Celibe	Figlio	deceduto a S.G.Persiceto il 8.5.1879
4	MONTANARI ADELE di " "	S.G.Persiceto	8.5.1868	Cg.Malferrari Ernesto	Figlia	deceduta a S.G.Persiceto il 6.3.1953
5	MONTANARI SATURNO di " "	S.G.Persiceto	20.4.1870	Cg.Vecchi Virginia	Figlio	emigrato a Springfield (USA) nel marzo 1913
6	MONTANARI LUIGI di " "	S.G.Persiceto	20.1.1872	Celibe	Figlio	deceduto a S.G.Persiceto il 29.8.1872
7	MONTANARI GIUSEPPE di " "	S.G.Persiceto	5.10.1873	Celibe	Figlio	deceduto a S.G.Persiceto il 18.1.1874
8	VECCHI VIRGINIA di Carlo e Collina Luigia	S.G.Persiceto	17.5.1875	Cg.Montanari Saturno	Nuora	emigrata negli USA il 28.10.1915
9	MONTANARI ALBERTO di Saturno e Vecchi Virginia	S.G.Persiceto	26.4.1892	Cg.Bonaveri Maria	Nipote	emigrato negli USA il 28.10.1915
10	MONTANARI FERDINANDO di Saturno e Vecchi Virginia	S.G.Persiceto	31.10.1896	Celibe	Nipote	emigrato negli USA il 29.10.1914
11	MONTANARI ADELE di " "	S.G.Persiceto	20.7.1901	Nubile	Nipote	emigrata negli USA il 28.10.1915

NOTE: I.S.= Intestatario della scheda di famiglia. Montanari Andrea è registrato come facchino e Montanari Saturno come falegname.

In carta libera per uso ___

S. Giovanni in Persiceto, li ___ DIC. 1999

Tipografia Litografia «IL TORCHIO».

PER IL SINDACO

Certificato di Stato di Famiglia for the family of Andrea Montanari, compiled in 1999 from the Registro di Popolazione of the town of Persiceto, Province of Bologna, Region of Emilio-Romagna. (Certificate courtesy of Marcia Iannizzi Melnyk.)

STATO DI FAMIGLIA STORICO DI BALBONI CARLO

già residente in Cento (fr. Renazzo) Stradello Borsa Fiappa n.484

REL.PARENTELA	COGNOME	NOME	PATERNITA'	MATERNITA'	LUOGO DI NASCITA	DATA DI NASCITA	STATO CIVILE	ANNOTAZIONI
INTERESSATO	BALBONI	CARLO	LUIGI	BREGOLI MARIA	CENTO (FR. RENAZZO)	1/05/1834	CG.CON RINALDI CARLOTTA	DECEDUTO IL 10/6/1881
MOGLIE	RINALDI	CARLOTTA	ANGELO	MICHELINI MARIA	RAVARINO (MODENA)	27/07/1839	CG.CON BALBONI CARLO	NON CENSITA NEL 1921
FIGLIA	BALBONI	MARIA	CARLO	RINALDI CARLOTTA	CENTO (FR. RENAZZO)	7/03/1870	NUBILE	EMIGRATA A FINALE EMILIA (MODENA) IL 25/08/1886
FIGLIA	BALBONI	EMMA MARIA	CARLO	RINALDI CARLOTTA	CENTO (FR. RENAZZO)	13/10/1873	NUBILE	EMIGRATA A BONDENO (FERRARA) IL 24/10/1896
FIGLIO	BALBONI	ROBERTO	CARLO	RINALDI CARLOTTA	CENTO (FR. RENAZZO)	22/08/1876	NUBILE	DECEDUTO IL 6/06/1885
FIGLIO	BALBONI	ALDO	CARLO	RINALDI CARLOTTA	CENTO (FR. RENAZZO)	2/04/1878	CELIBE	NON CENSITO NEL 1921
NIPOTE	BALBONI	BIAGIO	N.N.	BALBONI EMMA	CENTO	2/02/1895	CELIBE	NON CENSITO NEL 1921

CENTO LI 17/01/2000

COMPLETO DELLE GENERALITA' A NORMA DELL'ART. 3 LEGGE 2/5/1957 N.432

L'UFFICIALE D'ANAGRAFE DELEGATO TRENTINI CRISTINA

Certificato di Stato di Famiglia for the family of Carlo Balboni, compiled in 2000 from the anagrafe records for the frazione of Renazzo kept in the town hall of Cento, Province of Ferrara, Region of Emilia-Romagna. (Certificate courtesy Marcia Iannizzi Mehyk.)

Certificato di Residenza. The second type of family record you may request from the *municipio* of your ancestral *comune* is the *certificato di residenza* (certificate of residency). This is secured directly from the *ufficio di anagrafe*, not the *ufficio dello stato civile*. It is prepared from *anagrafe* records that document the people living in a particular residence. Those records are updated as changes occur—children born, for example, or moved to another *comune* of Italy, or to a foreign country, or residents died—as we have just noted above.

All citizens of Italy carry a *carta d'identità* (identification card), which gives their legal address. When issuing such a *carta d'identità*, the local *ufficiale di anagrafe* consults these same residency records.

Archivio di Stato (State Archives)

After *archivi comunali*, the record repository of greatest value for genealogical information is the *archivio di stato* in the *capo luogo* of the province where your ancestors lived.

Archivi di stato are public archives staffed by archivists and trained clerks who are prepared to help you access the records you seek. The professional staff cannot, however, be expected to conduct research for you, either by correspondence or in person. Limited funds, time and personnel preclude that. They will respond to queries about their repository's holdings, but will not do any searching for you in the collections. That's *your* job.

Access to Italy's *archivi di stato* is free to all researchers for historic purposes; researchers working on commercial projects, however, must pay a fee and obtain a written permit. Practically all *archivi di stato* have their own photocopying and microfilming services, or can provide such services through approved private agencies for a reasonable fee. The bureaucratic obstacle course the researcher must negotiate to access these services, though, may seem maddeningly convoluted and exasperating to Americans. But it can be mastered.

For one American genealogist's experience and advice, see "Lessons Learned in Italian Archives: What to Know Before You Go," by Suzanne Russo, AG (*Association of Professional Genealogists Quarterly*, vol. xvii, no. 2, June 2002: 61–65).

Bear in mind as you deal with Italian archivists that you are in *their* archives. They are extending a courtesy to you, a foreigner, and you should follow patiently and cheerfully whatever regulations, formalities and procedures they have put in place to safeguard their own precious patrimony. Show proper deference and exercise proper decorum. The impression *you* make may ease the way for other American genealogists in the future.

In the Mezzogiorno, *archivi di stato* may conserve not only the civil records described above, but also some of the religious records that will be described in Chapter 5. This is because substantial Church property was confiscated and secularized by the new government following Garibaldi's conquest in 1860. Since that time there has been a certain tension between some ecclesiastical and civil authorities regarding the restoration of Church records to their original repositories. The struggle waxes and wanes, depending on the personalities of the officials in office at any given moment, but seems never to be definitively resolved. *Archivi di stato* north of Naples may also hold a variety of religious records.

It has already been stated that there are 103 provinces in Italy. However, the total number of *archivi di stato*, plus the *Archivio Centrale* in Rome, is 95. The reason why nine provinces do *not* have archives is that they were created in 1994 from older provinces, in much the same way as U.S. counties have sometimes been carved out of pre-existing counties. Obviously, these new provinces have no old records to preserve—not yet, at least.

Presumably, after a couple of generations of record creation and accumulation, the new provinces will construct archives to house their own materials. For the time being, though, if you wish to search the historical records pertaining to any one of these nine areas, you will find them in the *archivio di stato* of the province in which the area was located *prior to 1994.*

There are several ways to familiarize yourself with the organizational structure and documentary holdings of Italy's ninety-five *archivi di stato*. First of all, the *Guida Generale degli Archivi di Stato Italiani* (*General Guide to the Italian State Archives*) is published in four volumes by the Ministero per i Beni Culturali e Ambientali (Ministry of Cultural and Environmental Affairs), the government agency responsible for administration of the archives and libraries of Italy. Taking the *archivi di stato* in alphabetical order, this *Guida Generale* describes each one's holdings. Every description includes a section on *"Archivi di Famiglie e di Persone"* ("Individual and Family Archives"), which are manuscript collections that contain substantial genealogical and biographical information about families of the province.

The Ministero per i Beni Culturali e Ambientali also publishes a set of twenty modest monographs under the colorful title *Itinerari Archivistici Italiani* (*Italian Archival Itineraries*). The first volume—*Organizzazione Archivistica* (*Archival Organization*)—describes the national archival system. The second—*Archivio Centrale dello Stato*—describes the central archives in Rome. Each of the eighteen others describes the *archivi di stato* located in each *regione* of Italy (Abruzzo and Molise are combined into one, and there appears to be none, as of this writing, for the Valle D'Aosta).

These superbly illustrated little books present a brief overview of the documentary materials in every archives. They also contain practical information regarding addresses, hours of operation, photocopying services and so forth.

The online equivalent of these official publications is the Italian archival system's beautiful website, **www.archivi.beniculturali.it** (see illustration of the home page on p. 122). Here you will find the addresses, phone numbers and hours of operation of all ninety-five *archivi di stato*, plus an alphabetical index to each one's collections, which describes very briefly the various records and the years they cover. The site also includes a complete copy of the *Guida Generale* explained above and other finding aids.

In addition, some of the *archivi di stato*—though not all—publish their own guides and indexes, and have their own websites, which provide more detailed information for those archives than does **www.archivi.beniculturali.it**. It is hard to imagine planning any research at all in Italian State Archives without making conscientious use of these invaluable websites.

Stato Civile. The *archivio di stato* contains *stato civile* kept prior to 1870. It was in 1806 that Napoleon Bonaparte decreed that all births, marriages and deaths be registered with civil authorities throughout the country.

In northern Italy the keeping of *stato civile* was initiated anywhere between 1806 and 1815. After the Congress of Vienna in 1815, however, when Italy reverted to its pre-Napoleonic status, some areas of the north discontinued keeping *stato civile* until 1870. In the central Italian *regione* of *Toscana* (Tuscany), the *stato civile* have been housed in the *archivio di stato* in Florence continuously since 1808. In the southern *regioni* of Abruzzo, Molise, Campania, *Puglia* (Apulia), Basilicata, Calabria and *Sicilia* (Sicily)—which once m i n i s t e r o   p e r   i   b e n i   e   l e   a t t i v i t à   c u l t u r a l i

ARCHIVI
Sistema Archivistico Nazionale

html news

l'amministrazione
archivistica
Archivi e Soprintendenze

gli strumenti
la Guida generale degli Archivi di Stato
i verbali del Consiglio superiore
le disposizioni sugli archivi negli antichi Stati

il patrimonio
documentario

(Undata)

biblioteca
la biblioteca digitale
le pubblicazioni

normativa

rinvii: i links

il sito
staff · materiali · statistiche · immagini

il forum

Home page of **www.archivi.beniculturali.it,** the website of the Italian state archival system. Every *archivio di stato* is discussed, with practical information for using it and an alphabetical index to its collections. Here you may learn what records each archives has, what years they cover and so forth.

comprised the Kingdom of the Two Sicilies—*stato civile* have been kept continuously from 1809 on the mainland and from 1820 in Sicily. All of the pre-1870 *stato civile* kept in *archivi di stato* are similar in form and content to those housed in the *archivi comunali* described above, and most were microfilmed during the 1980s for the Family History Library.

Note, however, that the pre-1870 *stato civile* for the northern *regione* of Trentino-Alto Adige, made up of the *provincie* of Bolzano and Trento, may sometimes be found in the custody of local priests rather than the *archivi di stato*. This is because this Tyrolean territory was under Austrian control prior to Italian unification, and the custom there since the sixteenth century was for the local priest to serve as the *ufficiale dello stato civile*. In many *comuni* of Tentino-Alto Adige, this tradition continued right up to 1870.

Allegati. In a few provinces—especially in the Kingdom of the Two Sicilies, but never in the north—an additional record source may be found among the pre-1870 *stato civile: allegati* or *processi matrimoniali* (annexed documents). *Allegati* are documents presented by the bride and groom when recording their *solenne promessa* in the *municipio*. They are kept in a separate volume in connection with (annexed to) the *atti di matrimonio*.

Allegati usually include birth or baptismal certificates for the two spouses; death or burial certificates when one or more of the parents of the bride or groom was deceased; and records of the bride and groom's previous marriages, and of the death of previous spouses. Such *allegati* are in volumes separate from the *atti di matrimonio* and are not always available on microfilm at the Family History Library. Sometimes, however, the fortunate family researcher will discover that the *allegati* have indeed been filmed along with the *atti di matrimonio*.

Registri degli Uffici di Leva. Shortly after the unification of Italy, military service became mandatory for all eighteen-year-old males. Since about 1870, therefore, *registri degli Uffici di Leva* (registers of the Offices of Conscription) have been kept.

These *registri* list the name, *comune* of birth, date of birth, parents' names and physical description of all young men eligible for the draft, together with an explanation of their military status—whether they ever served, deserted or were exempted, and so forth. The *registri* are divided into annual *classe di leva* (conscription classes or groups), each of which is indexed by the names of the draftees who composed that *classe di leva*—that is, the names of those men who turned eighteen since the previous *classe di leva*.

Registri degli Uffici di Leva are maintained by the *distretto militare* (military district)—a *provincia* may contain perhaps five or six *distretti militare*—and those created since World War I may still be in the custody of the *distretto militare* where they were created. But older *registri di leva* have been deposited in the *archivio di stato*.

To learn which *distretto militare* had jurisdiction over your ancestor's *comune*, consult one of the gazetteers discussed in Chapter 2 under "Maps and Gazetteers." Note, too, that draftee records may sometimes be found on the town level; so you might find a record of your ancestor's military status in the *archivio comunale* of his *comune*.

However, if all you know is your ancestor's *provincia*, *registri di leva* may be an especially valuable resource, for they contain his *comune* of birth. Search the indexes of all the *classe di leva* most likely to include your ancestor in all of the registers of the five or six *distretti militare* of your ancestor's *provincia*. This may be time-consuming, but the draft record you eventually find will yield your ancestral *comune* of origin. If you are seeking the birthplace of a female ancestor, you might search the indexes for her father's or brother's name.

Knowing only an ancestor's *regione*, though, is an insufficient basis for undertaking a search of *registri di leva*. It is just not specific enough.

Earlier records of military service, sometimes dating back to the late eighteenth century and containing more or less the same information as the *registri di leva*, are also kept in *archivi di stato*. These records cover the different Italian states, duchies and kingdoms at different periods of history, those of Tuscany being notably plentiful. Whether you find one pertaining to an ancestor of yours will depend on the many vagaries of historical research, not least of which are the level of your skills and the extent of your patience.

Minute, Atti e Bastardelli Notarili. Notaries have always been much more important and performed a much broader scope of legal services in Italy than in the United States. Italian law requires that marriage contracts and dowries, wills, real and personal property transactions, lawsuits of all kinds, including settlements of heirship and guardianship of orphans, and other legal matters be officially registered by a *notaio* (notary). Consequently, Italians find in their notarial records the same kinds of records that Americans find in their county courthouses.

From the late Middle Ages (generally the 1400s, but in some places as early as the twelfth century) through the early twentieth century, the *notaio's* role in Italian society remained substantially unchanged. His professional activity resulted in three different records of value to genealogists: *minute, atti* and *bastardelli*.

When the notary met with his clients, he wrote a *minuta* (rough draft) of the transaction to be recorded, including the names of the principals and the facts of the matter. From his *minuta* he prepared the actual *atto* (deed), which is the written record of the transaction. The notary kept his *minuta* and a copy of the *atto* for his own records, but deposited the original *atto* in the office of the *distretto notarile* (notarial district) where he was licensed. The deed was then considered legally registered.

For his own purposes the notary maintained a chronological list of the *atti* he prepared, with a few words defining the parameters of each *atto*. This list—known as *"bastardelli"* because the abstracts were "illegitimate" (that is, they did not constitute a legal document)—provided accessibility for the notary to his own work. When a notary retired, or died, his *minute* and *bastardelli* were usually passed on to his successor. When the new notary found he had no further need of these, he deposited them in the office of his *distretto notarile*.

The notarial deed on p. 127 (only the first two pages out of a total of six are shown) illustrates how rich in genealogical information such records are. Documents similar to this one may be found for scores of Italian-American families whose immigrant forebears relinquished their inheritance—as a gift or for remuneration—to relatives who remained in Italy.

Pictured here is the copy sent to the client in the United States. The cover reads, "Office of the Notary, Dr. Filippo Chiofalo, Messina, 25 Risorgimento Street, first floor," followed by his office and home telephone numbers. "No. 22294 of the Collection, Copy of the deed of Purchase and Sale, Contracted between Mrs. Salvatrice Rivoli, of unknown parentage [party of the first part], and Mrs. Stefana Currao, daughter of the deceased Andrea, and Mr. Stephano Lucà, son of the deceased Antonio [party of the second part], Dated 30 November 1935 (Year XIV [of the Italian Republic])."

Stefano Lucà and his wife, Stafana Currao, residents of Salice, a *frazione* of Messina, are sitting in the notary's of-

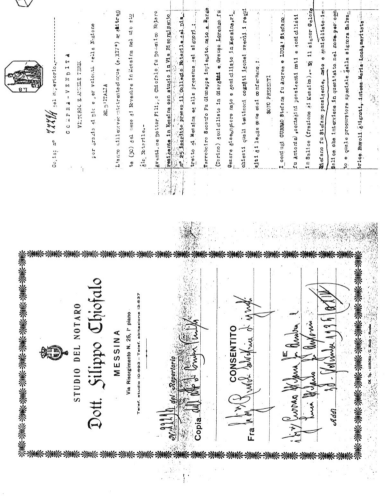

First two pages of an Italian notarial record dated 30 November 1935. The language and content of this deed of land transfer hardly vary from comparable notarial records of earlier centuries. *(From the collection of Louis Chibbaro.)*

fice with Stefano Celona, another resident of Salice who is representing the interests of Salvatrice Rivoli, who lives in New York City. Also present are two witnesses and, of course, the notary. Salvatrice Rivoli is a widow. Her husband—Stefano Lucà's uncle—has died, leaving her the portion of the Lucà family land he had inherited many years earlier. Since he was settled in America, he allowed his nephew, Stefano Lucà, to cultivate the land. Now Salvatrice is selling the property to the nephew.

All of this family history is made clear in the document. The land is described, as well as how and when Salvatrice's husband came to inherit a percentage interest in it. Note the use of the women's maiden names and the names of all parties' fathers, whether living or deceased, as further identification. Note also the arrangement of names, surname first, followed by given name. These practices are all very common in Italian records.

Notarial records of the past 100 years are still found in the possession of the individual notaries, in the files of district notarial offices or in archives—such as the *Archivio Notarile Distrettuale di Napoli* (District Notarial Archives of Naples)—that some populous notarial districts have had to create specifically for that purpose.

At the end of 100 years, however, the whole collection of *minute, atti* and *bastardelli* described above is transferred to the *archivio di stato*. These notarial records in *archivi di stato* may date back to the fourteenth century and sometimes even earlier.

In the *archivio di stato*, each notary's archives forms a separate collection, and the *bastardelli* serve as a kind of index to the collection. But remember, the *bastardelli* list the *atti* in chronological order and do *not* constitute a name index to the *atti*. In addition, the original *atti* that were deposited in the district notarial office by all of the notaries licensed in that district—perhaps fifty to eighty notaries—are also gathered into separate collections, one for each notary.

These notarial collections are arranged in chronological order by the registration date of each *atto, not* the date when the transaction occurred, and *not* by the names of the principals or the content of the *atto.* Therefore, if you do not know the name of the notary engaged by your ancestors to register their legal transactions, or at least an approximate date when any particular record you seek was registered, researching notarial records may be very time-consuming, as a page-by-page search through the collections of all of the notaries of a given district is required.

Depending on your research needs, however, the time may turn out to be wisely spent and may result in a wealth of information about the social and economic status of your ancestors. By their nature, notarial records are full of familial matters, relationships and dates, so that in some cases—when civil or religious records are lacking—they may be the only resource available for establishing a family group. To ignore them would be tantamount to ignoring the wealth of comparable records that fill county courthouses throughout the United States.

It is far from an easy task, however, to decipher the content of pre-twentieth-century notarial records once you have found them. Unlike the 1935 example discussed above, which is composed in standard Italian and neatly typed, older *atti* were written in a Latin jargon with its own abbreviations in a compact script called *gotico notarile* (notarial gothic). Unless your skills as a paleographer have been finely honed by this time in your research, you will have to hire a professional genealogist to decipher the old notarial records for you.

In rare and fortunate instances you may find notarial records that have been edited by scholars and printed in volumes specifically for historical research purposes. For example, in the *Archivio di Stato* in Trapani is the oldest register kept by an identified notary in Sicily. In 1943 it was transcribed into modern Italian, analyzed and published as *Il Registro Notarile di Giovanni Maiorana, 1297–1300* (*The Notarial Register of Giovanni Maiorana, 1297–1300*) by the historian Antonino de Stefano (see Bibliography). This volume is now available in the *biblioteca comunale* (municipal library) in Erice, the town near Trapani where the notary lived, as well as in other Italian libraries and the New York Public Library.

Notary records kept in Jewish communities throughout Italy are being edited and published by Shlomo Simonsohn (see the Bibliography and Chapter 5), and notary records kept in the Waldensian communities of Piedmont are available in the *Archivio di Stato* in Turin (see Chapter 5).

One final word regarding the notarial records of real estate transactions is appropriate here, as some familiarity with Italy's history and culture always helps genealogists understand and use the records created there. Historically, individual land ownership in northern Italy was much more common than in southern Italy. In the city states, duchies and kingdoms north of Rome, it was not uncommon for farmers to own their own modest farms. As landowners, they enjoyed a certain security, pride and social status.

By contrast, in the Kingdom of the Two Sicilies (today's Abruzzo, Molise, Campania, Basilicata, Apulia, Calabria and Sicily), most arable land was held in large plantations called *latifondi*. These huge estates were owned by aristocratic, noble and royal families (most of them non-Sicilian) and the Roman Catholic Church. The masses of men, women and children who labored in the fields lived the life of serfs beholden to their landlords for their livelihood, as well as for the administration of social justice and security. Do not be surprised, therefore, to find that your Calabrian ancestors, farmers for generations, never owned land.

Censimenti. National *censimenti* (population censuses) of Italy taken in 1861, 1871, 1881, 1891 and 1901 are available for searching in *archivi di stato*. Unfortunately, however, these censuses do not name every member of every family. Rather, they list heads of household with only statistical data for the other members of the household, similar to pre-1850 U.S. censuses (discussed in Chapter 3).

The later censuses of 1911—considered the first major national census—1921, 1931, 1936, 1951, 1961, 1971, 1981 and 1991 are much more informative. They enumerate the total population of Italy by family unit, including the names and ages of the husband, wife and dependent children, occupation of the head of household, and places of birth of all members of the family. However, these censuses are *not* open to the public.

You may request extracts from them, though, by writing to the *ufficio di anagrafe* in the *comune* of your ancestors. This has already been explained under "Certificato di Stato di Famiglia" and "Certificato di Residenza" on pp. 110–118. But you must be able to provide sufficient information to make the search feasible, and the *ufficiale di anagrafe* must be willing to undertake the assignment.

Many *archivi di stato* also hold an assortment of other censuses taken at various times in various localities. These date back to the middle of the eighteenth century, and the type and amount of information they show differs a great deal from one area of Italy to another. For example, censuses were taken in the *regione* of *Sardegna* (Sardinia) in 1848 and 1857. For years prior to about 1750, however, you must turn to parish censuses (these will be described later under *"Archivi Parrocchiali"*) or to *catasti* (tax assessment records or lists) for enumerations of family units.

Catasti. Italians have lived with a copious variety of tax obligations over the centuries, from taxes on land and houses to taxes on livestock and family members, and more. *Catasti*, therefore, are varied and voluminous.

Generally, *catasti* enumerate property owners and indicate their taxable property and the amount of tax assessed on it. Sometimes they include the names, or names and ages, of the property owner's household. They may be civil records or parish tithing records. They may date back as far as the fourteenth century or be as recent as the nineteenth century.

Some *catasti* are called *Riveli* (Declarations), which are lists of heads of household "declaring" or "revealing" the precise extent and nature of the taxable property they hold, including *beni mobili* (personal property) and *beni immobili* (real estate). *Riveli* are particularly useful because they include names of members of each taxpayer's household. However, they are also voluminous and require a time-consuming page-by-page search.

Catasti pertaining to the former Papal States—the present-day provinces of Ancona, Ascoli Piceno, Macerata and Pesaro-Urbino (the *regione* of *Marche*), Perugia and Terni (the *regione* of *Umbria*), and Frosinone, Latina, Rieti, Roma and Viterbo (the *regione* of *Lazio* [Latium])—are not kept in their respective *archivi di stato*. They are in the *Archivio Segreto del Vaticano* (Secret Archives of the Vatican), which means that accessing them is more troublesome (more about this below).

Catasti are especially useful sources of information about families that owned land, no matter how little. As already noted, ownership of modest pieces of private land was historically much more common north of Rome than in the Mezzogiorno, where most of the land was divided into huge *latifondi* owned by a few privileged families and the Church. The vast majority of people in the south were landless. Nevertheless, persons without real estate could still appear in *catasti* prepared for taxing personal estate, such as a "head tax" on members of the family.

Catasti, unfortunately—like notary records—are a difficult resource to use, since they are multifarious, written in arcane script and unindexed.

Registri dell'Emigrazione e Passaporti. Of particular interest to Americans tracing Italian ancestors, naturally, are records relating to emigration: 1) passport applications, and 2) departure lists. The disappointing truth of the matter is that Italy offers no documentary resources equivalent to the massive, information-packed, relatively uniform and indexed U.S. passport applications and passenger arrival records so readily accessible anywhere in the country on microfilm and in digitized formats (discussed in Chapter 3). Comparable records in Italy are much more diverse and dispersed and accessible only through diligent research *in situ*.

Prior to 1869 permits to emigrate were issued by regional heads of state—such as the King of the Two Sicilies in Naples, or the Duke of Tuscany in Florence—through a governmental agency. Since the unification of Italy, passport applications have been made at the local *questura* (police station). *Registri dell'Emigrazione e Passaporti* (Registers of Emigration and Passports) from about 1800 through World War I are preserved in *archivi di stato*, with those dated 1869 and later being among the records of the *Polizia* (Police) or *Prefettura* (Prefect). Passport records since World War I, however, are still in the custody of the *questura* where the application was made.

Emigration and passport records usually contain the following information: name of the emigrant, *comune* of birth, age or birth date, date when applying to emigrate or date when emigration will be permitted, and the port of departure and destination.

A separate set of records dealing with emigration matters has been kept since 1869 by the *Ministero dell'Interno* (Ministry of the Interior) in Rome, where they are maintained today—closed to public inspection. However, requests for genealogical information from these records may be granted if you make clear your relationship to the emigrant and give a reason for requesting the information that the ministry considers satisfactory.

Italian Emigration. Some knowledge of the history of emigration out of Italy may be helpful for locating and accessing Italian emigration records. Few Italians emigrated to the American colonies in the seventeenth and eighteenth centuries. Those who did sailed mostly from England or Holland in English or Dutch sailing vessels.

By the 1880s, however, when steam had displaced canvas for propelling passenger vessels across oceans, and Italian emigration to the United States was on the upswing, emigrants began sailing directly out of Italian ports on Italian steamships. Genoa, Naples and Palermo quickly became the busiest ports of departure. Emigrants tended to use the port most accessible to their *comune*. Those who lived in the north generally favored Genoa, though residents of the northeast and the Adriatic coast might use the Slovenian port of Trieste (annexed to Italy in 1918) instead. Those who lived in the Mezzogiorno used Naples and Palermo.

However, do not assume that because your ancestors were Italian they emigrated to the United States directly from Italian ports or sailed on Italian liners. By the late nineteenth century French and British steamships were sailing regularly from the ports of Italy. The French ports of Marseilles and LeHavre were also being used by some Italian emigrants who sailed on French liners. It was also not unheard of for an Italian to travel to Liverpool and take an English ship, or to Bremen or Hamburg and board a German vessel.

Steamship companies were linked to established routes, and Italians wishing to arrive at a particular U.S. port (say, to join relatives) had necessarily to use the port of embarkation serviced by a steamship line having that American destination. This would explain why a resident of Palermo, for instance, would opt to sail out of Naples or Messina, or even Marseilles, rather than his own city.

Steamship companies also vied fiercely for the lucrative emigrant business by offering competitive transatlantic fares and on-board accommodations. So Italians seeking a cheaper fare or better accommodations would select a steamship line accordingly. Often this meant *not* using the closest port of embarkation.

Archivio Centrale dello Stato (National Archives)

The *Archivio Centrale dello Stato* in Rome is the national repository for the historically valuable records created by the numerous agencies and offices of the Italian government. As already noted at the beginning of this chapter, these records document the official operations of the government and contain little information of genealogical interest. The *Archivio Centrale*, therefore, is the *last* civil archives of resort for genealogical research. For specific information about the holdings of the *Archivio Centrale* in Rome, consult the *Guida Generale degli Archivi di Stato Italiani* cited in the Bibliography, as well as **www.archivi.beniculturali.it**.

5. Religious Records of Italy

R ecords created by religious institutions throughout Italy are as useful to Americans researching their roots as are the records created by civil authorities described in Chapter 4. Often they are *more* useful, since the registration of baptisms, marriages and burials was initiated by the Catholic Church more than 200 years before the state started recording births, marriages and deaths. The vast majority of religious records in Italy are Roman Catholic. However, records of Jewish and Protestant communities are also available for research. All three will be discussed in this chapter.

Catholic Records

The Catholic tradition in Italy is ancient, powerful and pervasive. The country is divided into about 300 *diocesi* (dioceses; singular is also *diocesi*), which are composed of individual *parrocchie* (parishes; singular is *parrocchia*). The head of a *diocesi* is a *vescovo* (bishop); the head of a *parrocchia* is a *parroco* (pastor). Every *comune*, regardless of how small it may be, has its own *parrocchia*, and many *comuni* have more than one. In those cases one church is designated the town's *Chiesa Madre* (Mother Church)—sometimes called the *Chiesa Madrice* or, in the north, the *Duomo*. Even a *frazione* may support its own parish. Catholic records are found on both the parochial level and the diocesan level.

When corresponding with Roman Catholic parishes in Italy, it may be helpful to consult the *Annuario delle Diocesi d'Italia* (*Annual of the Dioceses of Italy*), which is available in larger research libraries. This book lists all of the Roman Catholic dioceses of Italy, naming each one's parishes and giving each parish's *comune, provincia* and pastor's name as of its year of publication (1951). For more current information, try searching on the Internet (some sites suggested in Chapter 2 under "Maps and Gazetteers"). In cities and larger towns with several parishes, finding the right parish may entail some trial and error, for parish boundaries have changed over the years.

Archivi Parrocchiali. Most Catholic Church records of interest to genealogists are still maintained in individual *Archivi Parrocchiali* (Parish Archives). Parish archives consist of the baptismal, marriage and burial registers, and the censuses of parishioners, recorded over the years by the priests.

The practice of keeping a written account of the administration of the sacraments of baptism, marriage and extreme unction was first proposed at the Council of Trent in 1562; it was ratified by the Pope in 1595. However, since the practice was slow to be enforced uniformly throughout Italy, most parishes will not have any records prior to the early seventeenth century (or even later, of course, if the parish was founded later). The earliest parish census will normally coincide with the founding of the parish.

Catholic Church records are handwritten in a "shorthand" Latin full of abbreviations, in Italian, or—in some areas of the north—in local dialect. Useful tools for deciphering the Latin and Italian abbreviations you will encounter in the old scripts of Italy are 1) Cappelli's *Dizionario di Abbreviature Latine ed Italiane* (*Dictionary of Latin and Italian Abbreviations*), and 2) Battelli's *Lezioni di Paleografia* (*Lessons in Paleography*), both cited in the Bibliography.

The informational content of baptismal, marriage and burial records, as well as parish censuses, varies a great deal from parish to parish, and older records generally provide much less information than do the more recent ones. Accuracy varies dramatically by locality and historic period. Parish registers survive in every conceivable state of preservation, from tattered volumes crumbling to pieces to handsomely bound volumes, from pages faded beyond deciphering to remarkably legible pages.

Atto di Battesimo. An *atto di battesimo* (baptismal record) contains the date the sacrament was administered, name of the priest who presided, name of his parish, date (and sometimes hour) of the infant's birth, name of the father and maiden name of the mother, place of residence of the parents, name given the infant and the names (and sometimes relationship or place of residence) of two godparents (see illustration on p. 140).

When the infant or parents are from another town, the name of that town is given. The entries in many baptismal registers are annotated in the margin with the date and place when the baptized infant married.

Atto di Matrimonio. An *atto di matrimonio* (marriage record) contains the date the sacrament was administered; name of the priest who presided; name of the parish; name of the groom and his parents, including his mother's maiden name (sometimes places of residence); name of the bride and her parents, including her mother's maiden name (sometimes places of residence); and the names (and sometimes relationship or places of residence) of two witnesses.

When the groom or bride is from another town, the name of that town is given. Traditionally, a couple is married in the bride's parish. Look there for the record. When either the groom or bride was married before, the name of the

Page from a typical Catholic baptismal register, recording that the baptism of Emilia Giuseppa Rosa Sorcino (number 11), daughter of Leopoldo and Artamisia Ottaviani, born the previous day, took place on 16 June 1831. Note that Catholic records are in Latin. (*Photograph courtesy of the Latter-day Saints Family History Library.*)

previous spouse is given, and sometimes the date and place of that first spouse's demise.

Atto di Sepoltura. An *atto di sepoltura* (or *atto di seppellimento, Decesso* or *Defunto*) (burial record or death record) generally contains the name and age of the deceased person, sometimes his or her parents' names, date of death, date of burial, and if the deceased was married, the name of his or her spouse, and whether that spouse is still living or not (see illustration on p. 142).

Women, whether single, married or widowed, are entered under their maiden name, and that is the surname you should look for in the index or marginal notation, *not* the husband's surname. Sometimes a widow's surviving husband is indicated as *secondo sposso* (second spouse), indicating that the woman had been married previously.

About 80 percent of the parish registers of the city of Rome are no longer retained in individual parish archives. They are deposited in the *Archivio Segreto del Vaticano* (Secret Archives of the Vatican), in the *Sezione Archivio del Vicariate di Roma* (Department or Branch of the Vicariate of Rome). Also, the parish registers of the *regione* of Umbria, and those of the *comuni* of Arezzo, Catania, Valdi and Lucerna, are retained in their respective *archivio diocesano* (diocesan archives).

Status Animarum. From around 1600 through the middle of the nineteenth century (depending on the locality; Papal States tend to be earlier than most), Italian parishes used to take a census periodically—sometimes annually, more often at irregular intervals—listing all parishioners by household, sometimes with ages, and indicating their familial relationships. Such a census is called in Latin *Status Animarum* (State of Souls) or simply *Animae* (Souls); in Italian it is a *Stato delle Anime* or simply *Anime*; and in English it is generally referred to as a Parish Census or Clerical Survey.

Page from a typical Catholic burial register, recording that Lorenzo Rossi (number 4) died on 14 February 1812 at the age of about 18 and was buried the following day. (*Photograph courtesy of the Latter-day Saints Family History Library.*)

In parishes where these old clerical surveys have been retained, they may be found among the registers in the *archivio parrocchiale*. They are invaluable for reconstructing families from the seventeenth, eighteenth and nineteenth centuries, when it was not unusual for three generations to live under the same roof. They also facilitate interpreting the baptismal, marriage and burial records of the parish.

In a few instances a parish census has found its way into an *archivio di stato,* and The Church of Jesus Christ of Latter-day Saints was able to microfilm it along with the civil records there. That microfilm is accessible to the lucky family historian through the Family History Library in Salt Lake City.

Archivi Diocesani. Individual dioceses also maintain an archives with holdings that record primarily the official actions of the bishop. These are called either *archivi diocesani* (diocesan archives) or *archivi vescovili* (bishop's archives).

Confirmation records, which may date back to the early seventeenth century, are found here, since it is the bishop who administers the sacrament of confirmation. These registers list the names of people confirmed, dates of their confirmations and sometimes the names of their sponsors.

Records of dispensations granted by the bishop—for a marriage between first cousins, for instance, or a marriage between a Catholic and a Protestant—show the names of the intended spouses, their residences, the date and nature of the dispensation, and sometimes even a pedigree chart to illustrate the degree of consanguinity.

Records of converts to the Catholic Church include the converts' names, residences and ages. There are also records of excommunication, since a bishop may excommunicate from the Church a parishioner of his diocese.

Archivi diocesani often hold the membership records of various Catholic confraternities, institutions and charity organizations, as well as biographical information about the bishops, priests and other Church officials of the diocese.

Other registers in an *archivio diocesano* could include records of the administration of the diocese, such as the purchase and sale of Church land, accounts of tenants working and living on Church land, the founding and closing of parishes, and so forth, as well as the *archivi parrocchiali* of defunct parishes.

Registers labeled *legati* (legacies) list the names of individuals who willed property to the Church, together with a description of the bequest, or who left funds for annual Masses in remembrance of deceased family members, with the amount.

Finally, a diocesan archives often contains a duplicate record of every marriage performed in the diocese, together with baptismal certificates for the bride and groom.

The registers in an *archivio diocesano* may date back to the middle of the sixteenth century and come up to the present day. The more recent records are still in the custody of the diocesan archives, which may be attached to the bishop's residence or the mother parish of the diocese. But the older registers have sometimes been deposited in *archivi di stato*.

Archivi parrocchiali, archivi diocesani and the *Archivio Segreto del Vaticano* are the private archives of the Roman Catholic Church: they are *not* public research institutions. Americans have no moral or legal "right" to the information about their ancestors contained in the old registers of the Church. Access to that information is a privilege.

Access to an *archivio parrocchiale* is a courtesy extended by the pastor of the parish. Americans who have traveled to Italy to trace ancestors in *archivi parrocchiali*, or who have corresponded or tried to correspond with Italian priests, relate vastly different experiences. The reception you receive will vary from one parish to another. Most priests have no staff and are extremely busy not only with their regular liturgical and sacramental duties, but also with teaching school, working with youths, organizing community activities and so forth.

Nevertheless, this author's experience on several research trips to several different parishes has been positive. Access to the *archivi parrocchiali* was granted as long as I used them during the hours when the sacristy was normally open, and did not expect assistance from the priest. Parish priests are seldom trained historians or archivists. On the contrary, it is becoming increasingly common to encounter Church officials who can neither decipher nor translate the Latin script that fills the ancient ecclesiastical registers.

On only one occasion did I fail to gain access to a parish archives, and that was due more to logistical problems with the pastor's busy schedule than to any set policy. Not all Americans, though, have had similarly happy experiences.

Showing respect and deference when dealing with religious authorities in Italy is not only diplomatically expedient, but appropriate to the culture (for more on the importance of writing letters of introduction and understanding the cultural context, see Chapter 7). In addition, since access to a parish archives is a favor, it is common courtesy for a researcher to return the favor with equal kindness. Showing your appreciation by leaving a generous gift *"per i bisogni della parrocchia"* ("for the needs of the parish")— candles or flowers for the altar, a donation toward the restoration of the organ, a series of Masses for your ancestors—is an appropriate and deeply appreciated gesture.

I have never been charged a fee for a church record. On the other hand, an Italian priest would be delinquent in his responsibilities if he did not remind the American genealogist gaining information from his records that the parish has many needs and can always use a new source of revenue.

Access to an *archivio diocesano* is gained from the designated person on the bishop's staff. It is generally granted if, once again, the researcher displays proper attitude and decorum, ability and seriousness, flexibility and appreciation, and uses the archives during the hours when the episcopal office is normally open—and without constant assistance from the bishop's staff.

Access to the *Archivio Segreto del Vaticano*, on the other hand, is obtained from the appropriate official on the Pope's staff and is generally granted only to university professors and published scholars.

If you are unable to find the religious records you need, ask for the name and address of the local church historian or antiquary. This is the person—official or unofficial—who is most familiar with the whereabouts of the church records created in his or her province or region. Contact this person and ask for assistance.

Jewish Records

Jewish resources have survived that warrant mention, for they pre-date the Italian civil records already discussed in Chapter 4, and are therefore invaluable to Americans tracing Italian ancestors who were Jews. The Italian Jewish community, with its 2,000 years of history, was formed by the merger of several Jewish groups that arrived in Italy at different times.

The nucleus was formed by Jews who lived in Italy during the Roman Empire before the destruction of the Second Temple in Jerusalem in 70 A.D. They resided primarily in Rome and throughout the southern Italian peninsula and island of Sicily. Palestinian Jews arrived in southern Italy during the fourth, fifth and sixth centuries, and later moved north, forming the roots of the Ashkenazic branch of Judaism.

This concentration of Jews in northern Italy grew in the fourteenth century. Ashkenazic Jews, fleeing Germany because of the Black Plague (1348) and the Crusades, settled in the Piedmont and Veneto regions. French Jews expelled from that country in 1306 and 1394 also went to the Piedmont. And Jewish Italian bankers migrated north from Rome.

In 1492, when the Spanish monarchs King Ferdinand and Queen Isabella expelled all Jews who refused to convert to Christianity, the Kingdom of the Two Sicilies was a part of their realm. Many Jews fled Naples and Sicily then and, migrating northward into the Papal States, joined the Jewish community of Rome. Numerous others settled in the northern cities of Florence, Genoa, Leghorn (*Livorno*), Milan, Turin and Venice.

At the end of the fifteenth and during the sixteenth century, the Spanish Inquisition spurred Sephardic immigration from Spain and Portugal. Directly or via Holland and the Muslim countries, Jews came to the Papal States. They settled primarily in Rome and the northern cities of Ferrara, Modena, Reggio Emilia and especially Leghorn.

Finally, some Jews from the Ottoman Empire migrated to Italy in the late eighteenth century.

Only in Italy did Ashkenazic and Sephardic Jews mingle and marry, and in these prosperous urban centers Italian Jewry enjoyed a Golden Age during the Renaissance. At the same time, however, the first ghetto was established in Venice, followed by others in many of the smaller northern towns and villages.

The word "ghetto" is itself of northern Italian origin. Although its precise etymology is "hotly debated by historians and linguists," writes Riccardo Calimani in *The Ghetto of Venice* (see Bibliography), "the commonly accepted opinion is that *ghetto* is a Venetian word denoting an enclosed area where the Jews were obliged to live. In earlier times, the site occupied by the ghetto was the site of a foundry, called *geto* in Venetian dialect. . . . "

Many illustrious rabbinic families derive from this Golden Age of Italian Jewish culture. The Abravanel family, for instance, traces its proud history back to Venice, and the famous Luria family is believed to have taken its name from the northern Italian village of Loria.

Italian Jewry peaked in the seventeenth century at about 50,000 and has declined steadily ever since. By the end of the Holocaust, most of Italy's Jewish communities had disappeared. Today's population is estimated at about 35,000. One of the many destinations of emigrating Italian Jews has been the United States, and the descendants of these immigrants have a variety of resources available to trace their ancestry.

Jewish Patronymics and Surnames. Some Jews in Italy adopted hereditary surnames along with their non-Jewish neighbors as early as the tenth and eleventh centuries (making them the first in Europe to do so). Normally, they either translated their Hebrew name or assumed the name of their place of origin.

Other Italian Jews, however, continued to practice the ancient custom of patronymics, whereby an individual was identified by his or her given name and the given name of his or her father—Samuel ben Jacob, for example, or Sarah bar Benjamin. In the late eighteenth century, however, Napoleon decreed that all Jews adopt a fixed surname. At that time, some Italian Jewish families took as their surname the name of their town or city. Not *all* Jewish surnames, however, will lead directly to an ancestral town.

For pre-eighteenth-century research, therefore, knowing the *given* names of your ancestors becomes vital, because only their given names and patronymics will identify them. Knowing your ancestor's *comune* of birth also becomes especially critical, since only the particular place name following your ancestor's given name and patronymic will distinguish him or her from others with an identical name and patronymic. For instance, you might find in ancient notarial deeds "Isaac ben Abraham of Turin" and "Isaac ben Abraham of Novara," to distinguish between two Isaac ben Abrahams living in close proximity.

A useful work, particularly if you are uncertain of the native town of your family, is Samuele Schaert's *I Cognomi degli Ebrei d'Italia* (*Surnames of the Jews of Italy*). This book indicates the place of origin of many Italian Jewish surnames.

Jewish Local History. Prior to seeking original records, you should learn as much as possible from published materials about the Jews of your ancestral *comune*. Annie Sacerdoti's *Guida all'Italia Ebraica* (*Guide to Jewish Italy*) surveys, region by region, *comune* by *comune*, all of Italy's Jewish communities—those defunct and those still thriving. Sacerdoti provides a brief historical sketch of each community, followed by a description of its synagogue, cemeteries, and any museums, libraries or research centers devoted to Jewish history and culture. An English translation of this work exists (see Bibliography); however, its historical sketches are not as detailed as those of the original Italian edition.

There is an extensive corpus of Italian Jewish local history. For a bibliographic listing of recent works dealing with the history of the Jews in Italy, including works about particular localities and families, consult Aldo Luzzatto's *Biblioteca Italo-Ebraica* (*The Italo-Jewish Library*) and its supplement to 1995 by Manuela Consonni.

Substantial histories of individual Jewish communities—such as Riccardo Calimani's *The Ghetto of Venice* (cited above), or Shlomo Simonsohn's *History of the Jews of the Duchy of Mantua*—are often published in English. These histories usually contain a lengthy bibliography of related works, which will direct you to additional secondary literature as well as documentary sources valuable for your family research. The histories are also indexed by personal name, and some, such as Simonsohn's, are indexed by place names and subjects too.

Published Genealogies. To exploit the resources available in American libraries, you should also try to discover whether a genealogy of your family has already appeared in print. Nello Pavoncello has begun a series of books titled *Antiche Famiglie Ebraiche Italiane* (*Ancient Italian Jewish Families*). Volume I, published in 1982, contains the histories of twenty families reprinted from articles appearing between 1957 and 1960 in the *Settimanale Israel* (*Israel Weekly*). But no subsequent volume has yet appeared.

Sometimes the genealogy of a Jewish family will appear as part of a larger work. For example, Vittore Colorni's *Judaica Minora: Saggi sulla Storia dell'Ebraismo Italiano dall'Antichità all'Età Moderna* (*Judaica Minora: Essays on the History of Italian Judaism from Antiquity to Modern Times*) (Milan: Dott. A. Giuffre, Editore, 1983) includes two essays that trace two prominent Jewish families—Finzi and Colorni—generation by generation, from the fifteenth century to the present day.

Less detailed Jewish family histories appear in "Parnassim: Le Grande Famiglie Ebraiche Italiane dal Secolo XI al XIX" ("Parnassim: The Great Italian Jewish Families from the Eleventh to the Nineteenth Century"), by Franco Pisa. This series of articles appeared from 1980 through 1984 in the *Annuario di Studi Ebraici* (*Annual of Jewish Studies*), edited by Ariel Toaff.

Of course, some Jewish family histories may also appear in the general bibliographies of Italian genealogy discussed under "Genealogies of Titled Families" in Chapter 2.

Journals. Another way to prepare to search for Jewish forefathers in Italian records is to read pertinent journals—those about Italian genealogy in general already discussed in Chapter 1, as well as those that focus specifically on Jewish genealogy, such as *AVOTAYNU, the International Review of Jewish Genealogy*, *Dorot*, and *SEARCH*.

For example, *POINTers*, the quarterly journal of POINT (Pursuing Our Italian Names Together), published an article by Dale Leppart in the Summer 1991 issue. In the article, titled "Researching a Judaic Family in Italy," Leppart relates his surprise at discovering Jewish ancestors in his Italian family tree. From the time of the Spanish Inquisition to the present day, generation to generation, the family had guarded the secret of its Jewishness.

"The Ghetto of Verona," by Mark Tedeschi, appeared in *AVOTAYNU* in the Fall 1988 issue. His article provides research information and advice based on his own experience tracing ancestors in Verona.

"Italian Research," by Marsha Saron Dennis, appeared in *Dorot*, the newsletter of the Jewish Genealogical Society, Inc., in the Autumn 1989 issue. Based on her own experience, Dennis offers advice on what to do, and what *not* to do, to ensure success in your research trip to Italy.

The quarterly titled *SEARCH*, published by the Jewish Genealogical Society of Illinois, also contains pieces on Italian Jewry from time to time.

Websites. American Jews tracing their Italian roots should take full advantage of the well-developed and wonderfully informative network of Internet websites devoted to Jewish genealogy. An excellent starting point is **www.jewishgen.org**. The links from there will take you far into your investigation of your Jewish heritage.

Writing to the Jewish Community. After you have
learned the *comune* of your ancestors, write a letter to the
Jewish community or rabbi there. If none of the resources
cited above gives you the rabbi's name and address, consult *The Jewish Travel Guide*, published annually by Jewish
Chronicle Publications (25 Furnival Street, London EC4A
1JT, England). It lists all extant organized Jewish communities around the world and provides addresses.

The rabbi of your ancestors' *comune* will be able to in-
form you of the extent and location of surviving records
for his community. If your ancestors' community has disappeared, as most of the smaller ones have, write to the
rabbi of the closest synagogue still in existence.

Records of birth, marriage and death have survived for
many Jewish communities and may date back as far as the
seventeenth century. These are usually kept in the local
synagogue, but may be part of the *archivio comunale* (see
below). The rabbi will also know whether there is a Jewish
museum, library or research center in your ancestor's
comune. You will want to send a letter there as well.

Civil Repositories. In addition to the civil records already described in Chapter 4, *archivi comunali* and *archivi
di stato* often hold a miscellaneous assortment of records
relating specifically to Jews. These may include registra-
tions of Jewish births, marriages and deaths for a particular *comune*, as well as substantial documentation on local
rabbinical families.

Some notarial records dating back to the fourteenth century (sometimes even earlier) deal with the legal transactions, court cases, inheritance disputes, and other matters
involving Jews. In *The Jews of the Duchy of Milan*, four volumes published in 1986, Shlomo Simonsohn has printed—
in English translation, with notes and commentary—all of
the Jewish notarial records for the area around Milan from
the Middle Ages through the sixteenth century.

Special census enumerations were often made of the inhabitants of Jewish ghettos too. In the *Archivio di Stato* in Verona, for example, is a manuscript book from 1776, which contains a detailed description of the Jewish ghetto of that city. It includes a map of the ghetto and a house-by-house listing that gives not only the occupants' names, but also their occupations.

Catholic Repositories. Since a large portion of Italy's Jewish population has lived for centuries—especially since 1492—in the area that comprised the Papal States, various records pertaining to Jews can also be found in the *Archivio Segreto del Vaticano. Catasti* (tax records, discussed in Chapter 4) are one of these. Unfortunately, access to Vatican archives is not easily secured.

University Records. Jews have occupied influential and much-respected positions in the universities of Italy. Therefore, *registri delle università* (university registers) may also prove valuable to Jewish genealogy. These are explained in Chapter 6.

Cemeteries. A trip to your ancestor's *comune* will allow you to exploit a resource not available in American libraries or through correspondence (unless you have a researcher working for you in Italy): cemeteries. Jewish cemeteries in Italy are unlike Christian cemeteries (see Chapter 7) insofar as the individual graves, with their individual headstones, are maintained in perpetuity. Some of the older cemeteries were destroyed years ago, but many are still maintained. So you may be able to use names and dates inscribed on cemetery monuments to extend your family tree. In some instances, however, monuments dating back to the seventeenth century and earlier bear only the name of the deceased, and no date of birth or death.

Centers for Jewish Studies. Finally, Americans seeking Jewish ancestors who were Italian should not overlook the collections housed in five major centers for Jewish studies, two in Italy and three in Israel.

The Centro di Documentazione Ebraica Contemporanea (Center for Contemporary Hebrew Documentation) (via Eupili 8, 20145 Milano) is Italy's only institution dedicated to Holocaust research. Its library holds thousands of studies of particular Jewish communities and families, over 1,500 Italian and foreign periodicals, original historical documents and newspaper clippings relating to the twentieth-century experience of Italian Jews, particularly during the Fascist era and World War II. The Center's website is **www.cdec.it.**

In Rome, the Centro Bibliografico (Bibliographic Center) of the Union of Italian Jewish Communities (Lungotevere Sanzio 5, 00153 Roma) holds published and original materials pertaining to Italian Jewish communities.

The Centro di Studi sull'Ebraismo Italiano (27 Hillel Street, Jerusalem), under the direction of Miriam Della Pergola, holds 6,000 books on Italian Jewry and many journals with articles on the Jewish communities of Italy. The Center is a part of Jerusalem's V. Nahon Museum of Italian Jewish Art (**www.italcham.org.il/museum/italindex.html**).

The Manuscript Department at the Jewish National and University Library (Hebrew University-Edmond Safra campus, Givat Ram, Jerusalem) holds several manuscripts from Italy. In the Microfilm Department are two *pinkassim* from the Vernadsky collection in Kiev, a Milan Jewish birth register, 1792–1831, and a late-nineteenth-century *pinkas* of the *chevra kadisha* from Siena. The Library's website is **www.jnul.huji.ac.il.**

At The Institute for Diaspora Research (Tel Aviv University, Ramat Aviv, Tel Aviv 69978), Professor Shlomo Simonsohn is devoting himself to publishing a complete documentary history of the Jews in Italy. His books of

Milan's notarial records (cited on p. 152) constitute part of that project. See the Institute's website at **http://www.tau.ac.il/humanities/institutes-index.html#diaspora**.

In 1492, when many Italian Jews migrated north of Naples because of the Spanish Inquisition, others immigrated to other lands. In subsequent centuries a number of these same families, experiencing persecution or facing expulsion by royal decree, removed yet again to the United States. Consequently, American Jews may trace their ancestors back to Italy via some intermediate country. Then, using the resources of Italy, they may discover that their Jewish ancestors originally migrated into the Italian peninsula or Sicily from any one of numerous *other* countries of both West and East.

So your *Italianità* may turn out to be only one chapter in the larger tome of your Jewish heritage. Your searching is not over yet!

Protestant Records

The number of Protestants in Italy has always been small—smaller than the number of Jews—and the Protestant population has historically been concentrated in an area in the Alps called the Waldensian Valleys. However, although Protestants have made up only a tiny fraction of the total Italian population, the majority of Italian immigrants to the United States prior to 1820 were Waldenses (as noted in the Introduction). For the descendants of these early immigrants who are researching their Protestant Italian roots, therefore, a description of the most important resources to consult is in order.

Waldenses. The Waldenses were followers of Peter Waldo, a twelfth-century separatist whose teachings were essentially "Protestant" three centuries before the Reformation. The majority of Waldenses lived in several inaccessible valleys in the Alps in the *regione* of *Piemonte* (Pied-mont), about thirty miles southwest of *Torino* (Turin)—an area that flip-flopped many times over the centuries between French and Italian domination. They managed to remain a cohesive and isolated religious sect out of the disciplinary reach of the Roman Church until the sixteenth century, when the Waldenses aligned with the Protestant Reformation.

A century of persecution and religious wars followed, which failed to eliminate the Waldenses, and freedom of worship was finally granted to them by law in 1848. In 1900 the Waldensian Valleys, the Pinerolo District and the city of Turin contained a population of perhaps 22,500 Waldenses divided into seventeen parishes. That same year the total number of Protestants in Italy—resulting from the missionary efforts of Baptist, Methodist, Seventh-Day Adventist and other Protestant ministers who started arriving in the 1860s—was around 33,000.

To this day Waldenses (perhaps 25,000 to 35,000 strong) remain the vast majority of Protestants in Italy. Recently they united with the Baptists and Methodists to form the *Chiesa Evangelica Italiana* (Italian Evangelical Church), with headquarters in Rome.

Records of the Protestant parishes of Italy are similar in content to those of the Catholic parishes, and they are also still in the custody of the individual parishes. The Family History Library has microfilmed the registers of sixteen Waldensian parishes in the Pinerolo District (see illustration on p. 157). These contain entries from about 1685 to the twentieth century. The registers of eight other Waldensian parishes that could not be filmed are currently being transcribed by hand.

Also available from the Family History Library are forty-three rolls of microfilm that constitute what is called the

Page from a marriage register of a Waldensian parish in the *comune* of Torre Pellice, *provincia* of Torino, recording that on 9 April 1750, Jean Bonjour, son of Daniel (deceased), married Marie Baridon, daughter of Daniel (deceased) and widow of Philippe Garoupin, Sr. Note that our records are in French and the names are French, reflecting the fact that this area in the Alps was at times under French dominion. Note, too, the use of the Italian term *"fu."* (*Photograph courtesy of the Latter-day Saints Family History Library.*)

"Piedmont Project." These rolls contain hundreds of family group sheets compiled from the microfilmed parish registers, as well as an alphabetical surname index to them.

It is noteworthy that the *Archivio di Stato* in Turin has Waldensian notarial records beginning in 1610. For their possible genealogical value, see the description of *Minute, Atti e Bastardelli Notarili* in Chapter 4.

Non-Italian Protestants. Many of Italy's Protestant parishes were founded and are maintained to this day for the benefit of foreign residents—diplomats, business people, writers, artists and so forth. Revalee Stevens, herself an American residing in Italy, has begun a series of books transcribing records pertaining to Protestant Americans in Italy. *North American Records in Italy: The Protestant Cemetery of Rome* contains the burial records and monument transcriptions of all Americans interred in Rome's Protestant Cemetery. *Protestant Records in Italy: The Registers of St. Paul's Within-the-Walls* contains the baptismal, marriage and burial records of American citizens in the registers of Rome's largest Protestant church.

Whether your Italian ancestors turn out to be Catholic, Jewish or Protestant, a cornucopia of religious resource material, both primary and secondary, is available to help you climb your family tree.

6. Libraries and Other Resources in Italy

Besides civil and religious archives, Italy has other repositories of resource materials useful to Americans pursuing Italian genealogical research. These include, most importantly, Italy's *biblioteche* (libraries). But several other kinds of specialized collections will also be described in this chapter.

Biblioteche (Libraries)

Italy has a well-organized national system of *biblioteche pubbliche statali* (state public libraries). There is no single "national library" analogous to the Bibliothèque Nationale in Paris or the Library of Congress in Washington. Rome, Florence, Bari, Milan, Naples, Potenza, Palermo, Turin and Venice all have a *biblioteca nazionale* (national library). Each one is named for an illustrious Italian—for example, the Biblioteca Nazionale Vittorio Emanuele III in Naples—and collects and preserves materials relating to its own area within Italy. All house not only published volumes, but also many manuscript collections of personal and family papers donated or bequeathed by local families.

The libraries of Rome and Florence hold the elevated status of *Biblioteca Nazionale Centrale* (Central National Library), because they serve as depository libraries for all printed matter published in Italy, as well as foreign works pertinent to Italian civilization.

In addition to these *biblioteche nazionali*, there are smaller libraries in other provincial capitals called *biblioteche statali* (state libraries), a number of specialized libraries (each one has its own name), and a dozen university libraries (*biblioteche universitatie*). University libraries are located in Bologna, Cagliari, Catania, Genoa, Messina, Modena, Naples, Padua, Pavia, Pisa, Rome and Sassari and are meant to support the research and study needs of the faculty and students there.

The best introduction to Italy's state public libraries is **www.librari.beniculturali.it** (see illustration on p. 161). Click on *servizi* (services), then click on *biblioteche*. A map of Italy showing the twenty regions will appear. Click on the region of interest to you, and a new screen will pop up with a map showing the provinces of that region and a list of the state libraries located there, with each one's city.

Click on any library and an informative website will provide the library's designation (national, state, university, etc.), director's name, address, telephone and fax numbers, e-mail address, hours of operation and a detailed history of the library. Some library catalogs may also be searched online.

Besides state libraries, Italy has hundreds of *biblioteche comunali* (local libraries). These are managed by the government of the *comune* and include materials on local history and genealogy.

Two guides found in American libraries, one in Italian, the other in English, are helpful for using Italian libraries. Francesco Marraro's *Repertorio delle Biblioteche Italiane* (*Repertory of Italian Libraries*) is a listing by region, and thereunder by province, of all of Italy's libraries (as of the book's date of publication). It includes the address and hours of each library, as well as the number of volumes and periodicals each one holds.

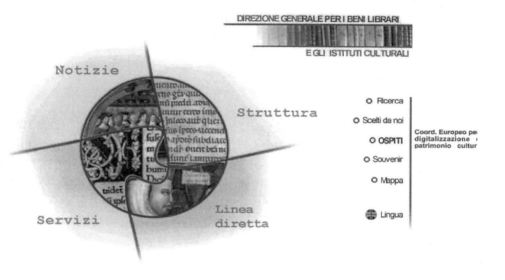

Sito ottimizzato perIE4 e NN4 - ris. 800x600

Notizie | Servizi | Struttura | Linea diretta
[Ricerca] [Scelti da noi] [Ospiti] [Souvenir] [Mappa] [Lingua inglese]

Home page of **www.librari.beniculturali.it,** the website of Italy's state library system. Every state *biblioteca* throughout the twenty regions of Italy is discussed, with practical information for using them. Note, however, that *biblioteche comunali*—local public libraries—are not part of the state system; each *biblioteca comunale* is managed by the government of the *comune* it serves. Private libraries are also not part of the state library system.

The Guide to Italian Libraries and Archives, compiled by Rudolf J. Lewanski, is intended specifically for American researchers and offers practical information about Italy's libraries and archives, as well as an overview of the entire national system. The practical information includes rules and regulations governing admission, hours of operation, photocopying and so forth, which vary from one library to the next throughout Italy.

Archivi Genealogici (Genealogical Archives)

Genealogical archives are collections of published and original materials pertaining to royal and noble families and to the clergy. These may be found as a separate collection or department in Italy's *archivi di stato*, or in any one of the *biblioteche pubbliche statali*, or sometimes even in *biblioteche comunali*. *Archivi genealogici* contain heraldic, ecclesiastical and genealogical materials, sometimes dating back to the twelfth century.

The head of a noble family was literally the ruler of his estates, on which there were towns and villages. The noble was lawmaker and judge to the men, women and children who populated his towns and villages and worked his land. So *archivi genealogici* contain not only the acts and judgments of the heads of titled families regarding all kinds of political, judicial and administrative matters, but also pedigree charts and coats of arms.

Americans who trace their ancestry back to a titled family of Italy will find their family histories already published and available in the libraries of Italy. These published genealogies have already been described in Chapter 2 under "Genealogies of Titled Families." Rarely, however, do *archivi genealogici* contain anything of family history value to descendants of Italy's *popolino*.

Archivi Ecclesiastici (Ecclesiastical Archives)

Ecclesiastical archives are collections of materials regarding the clergy of the Church. They include a variety of documents dating back to the thirteenth century that detail the names of members of the clergy, sometimes with birth dates, birthplaces and family relationships. *Archivi ecclesiastici* may be found in *archivi di stato*, the *Archivio Segreto del Vaticano* and sometimes *archivi diocesani*.

Registri delle Università (Registers of Universities)

If an ancestor of yours was a scholar, you may wish to consult the *Registri dell' Università* (registers of a university) where he or she studied or taught. Such registers may be found either in *archivi di stato* or at the university itself, and they may date back to the thirteenth century, as do those of Padua and Bologna, two of the oldest universities in the world.

Registri delle università (registers of universities) are generally kept by school, so it is helpful to know not only what university your ancestor may have been associated with, but whether he or she was in the school of medicine, law, theology, history, philosophy and so forth. Student records tend to be indexed by surname for each freshman class, however, and that makes using them a possible task regardless of how much prior knowledge you bring to the search.

After locating your ancestor in the index, you may consult his or her admission record, which provides the freshman's name, birth date and birthplace, as well as his or her father's name and occupation. When you are certain, based on this information, that you are dealing with the right student, consult his or her academic file. It will provide complete information about his or her scholarly activities at the university. There are also registers with information about instructors.

The genealogical boon of *registri delle università* is that when you find one ancestor, you often discover other family members there too, sometimes for succeeding generations. The limitation of these registers is, of course, that very few men and almost no women attended university in Italy prior to the late twentieth century. Advanced education in the arts and sciences was a prerogative of the scions of wealthy, usually titled, families.

Genealogical Institutes in Italy

It has already been stated in Chapter 2 that Italians who engage in genealogy tend to be men and women descended from families bearing titles and coats of arms. The genealogical institutes in Italy, therefore—similar to the *archivi genealogici* discussed above—tend to focus on ancient noble and royal lineages and their heraldry.

The largest genealogical institute in Italy is the *Istituto Genealogico Italiano* (Italian Genealogical Institute) (Via Santo Spirito 27, 50125 Firenze), which was founded in 1877 as the *Ufficio Araldico Italiano* (Italian Heraldic Office). Its website at **www.genealogia.it** explains the institution's history and mission, and offers its products and services.

One on-going project of this institution is the preparation of a general index to all manuscripts in Italy dealing with genealogy and heraldry. To date, the index includes about four million surnames and 200,000 coats of arms. You may contact the director of the *Istituto Genealogico Italiano* through the website for specific information about his collections. He will not conduct research for you but will let you know if your family's surname appears in the index.

Two other genealogical institutes, however, include American-born staff who have resided in Italy for many years. They advertise in U.S. genealogical periodicals and have conducted a great deal of research for Americans.

The Italian Genealogical & Heraldic Institute (Via Massimo d'Azeglio 9-B, 90143 Palermo) is under the direction of the Very Reverend Lawrence Casati and Cav. Luigi Mendola. The website of Luigi Mendola, a distinguished heraldist, has already been discussed in Chapter 2 under "Internet Websites." The website for the Institute is **www.regalis.com/institute.htm**.

The Italian Genealogical Institute (Via Modigliani, 1B, 35020 Albignasego, Padova) is operated by Trafford R. Cole, Ph.D., an Accredited Genealogist and author of numerous works in English on Italian genealogy (see Bibliography).

Aside from these institutes, however, individual Italians have begun to advertise their genealogical research services in American journals. Continued interest among Americans to learn more about their roots overseas has fostered a new industry for entrepreneurial Italians. One researcher who advertises that he operates throughout Italy, though he specializes in Abruzzo and Molise, is Sebastiano Pasquini. He, as well as others, may be reached via the Internet. However, since these services are relatively new and no body of evidence has yet been gathered to evaluate them critically, no more specific information about them is provided here. Always ask for references when employing a professional researcher.

7. Practical Suggestions for Success

Finding and using the Italian records that pertain to your family may take considerable time and effort. You want to be sure to reap the greatest harvest from your labors. Here are a few practical suggestions to help you get to the records you want, then understand fully the information they contain. Heeding these observations will not only facilitate your research, but result in a family history that is rich in *Italianità* as well.

Letters Open Doors

The necessity of corresponding with Italian repositories has already been mentioned several times. Nevertheless, the value of writing initial letters of introduction, and good, concise business letters in general, cannot be overemphasized. The following suggestions pertain equally to paper correspondence, e-mail messages, faxes and even telephone calls.

First of all, let the archivist, the pastor of the parish or the clerk in the town hall know who you are and what records you expect to find in his repository. Ask the days and hours of operation, whether photocopying is allowed, and any other practical information you will need to visit the repository in person. Such letters are appreciated by Italian officials, who would rather *you* come and do the research than ask *them* to do it.

The responses you receive will either confirm or correct your expectations and help you schedule your precious time. If you take them with you, the written replies serve as handy "door openers" when you arrive at the threshold of the institution—they already know you!

Italiano, si! Inglese, no!

English is not spoken by every Italian, as you may have been led to believe. True, many priests, clerks, archivists and librarians *can* "get by" in English when they have to. Usually, though, they remember only a few words and idioms from school days (or American films), which tend to be useless when communicating about historical research. Many Italians have trouble providing clear information or instruction in English. The best policy is to write in Italian.

Sample letters in Italian addressed to both civil and religious archives, with English translations, are readily available. They may be found in the works of Cole and Konrad cited in the Bibliography; in *POINTers*, vol. 5, no. 4, Winter 1991; and at the Internet sites of the Family History Library (**www.familysearch.org**), Il Circolo Calabrese (**www.circolocalabrese.org**) and *Italian Genealogy Homepage* (**http://italiangenealogy.tardio.com/html**).

You might turn to an elderly relative, neighbor, local librarian or Italian teacher, or fellow members of your genealogical society to help you draft letters in Italian and translate the replies that arrive from Italy. Professional translation services are also available. Peruse any popular bimonthly magazine, such as *Family Tree, Ancestry, Heritage Quest, Family Chronicle* and *Family History*, or any Italian genealogical society journal, such as *POINTers* or *Lo Specchio*, and you will see the advertisements of several Italian translators. Many libraries with genealogical collections subscribe to these publications and keep the back issues.

Furthermore, as stated at the outset, you will need to acquire at least a fundamental proficiency in the Italian language for your research to be successful and your appreciation of your Italian heritage to be more than superficial. At a minimum, use an English-Italian dictionary to familiarize yourself with a few key phrases of politeness, and learn the terms for the records you will be seeking. The glossary in this book is intended to help you get started and direct you to more extensive glossaries available elsewhere.

By all means, if you make a research trip to Italy, take an English-Italian/Italian-English dictionary with you. You can always point!

If, however, you have no choice but to write in English, compose short, simple sentences and be as brief and precise as possible. Address only one matter in each letter, not several matters involving several branches of your family. Complex letters overwhelm the recipient and tend to end up sitting in a dusty stack of papers on a desk.

The reply you receive may be written in Italian, broken English, fluent English . . . or, on occasion, you may get no reply at all. But the simpler and clearer your request, the more likely it will be answered.

Get All the Goods

Whether you write in Italian or English, when requesting civil records be sure to ask for the *atto integrale* (complete record). Otherwise the official will send you a short-form certificate in standard use throughout the European Union that does not include parents' names and may lack information contained in the original.

Postal Courtesy Makes Friends

You may wish to enclose a couple of international postal reply coupons with your letters. Italian postage is expensive—rates there are about twice what ours are—and these coupons may be redeemed by the recipient in Italy to pay the postage of the reply letter. This gesture shows that you are courteous, and serious and conscientious about your research. You should not expect *them* to foot the bill for answering *your* query. Obtain international postal reply coupons at your local post office.

On the other hand, many Americans have found that recipients in Italy do not bother to redeem these coupons because of the red tape involved. So you may opt instead to include a little extra money for postage when you send funds to Italy to pay for services and documents.

Send Money, But Not Cash!

When writing to civil archives or libraries, as a courtesy, offer to pay whatever fee may be required for the service. When writing to a priest, enclose a gift "for the church" (as discussed in Chapter 5 under "Archivi Parrocchiali"). But never send cash.

It is easy to obtain a draft check in Euros. Simply contact Thomas Cook Currency Services, Inc. (1-800-287-7362) or International Currency Express (**www.foreignmoney.com**). A check in the amount you specify, made payable to whomever you specify, will be mailed to you. Your payment for the check—which includes a service fee, of course—may be made by MasterCard or Visa or personal check.

The most economical and convenient way to pay for records and services from Italy is probably by credit card. But that mode of payment, unfortunately, is not always an option. Use it whenever you can.

Props Are Worth a Thousand (Italian) Words

When visiting the towns of your ancestors, as valuable as mastering a basic vocabulary of Italian words is taking along a family tree chart . . . which is worth a *thousand* Italian words. The chart should be simple, showing direct lines of descent only. You might even order blank pedigree charts and family group sheets printed in Italian from the Family History Library.

Displaying your chart to the villagers strolling in the *piazza* (town square), waiting at the bus stop or gossiping in the market, as well as to the curators of the repositories you visit, will make clear what you are doing and what you need. The villagers, if only to satisfy their curiosity, will pay attention to you and offer assistance.

Taking old family photographs (copies, of course, not the originals!) is also a good idea. These visual props sometimes jog a local citizen's memory and may lead you to distant kin still residing in your ancestral *paese*.

Culture Is More Than Language

Being able to translate into English the words found in an old Italian record is not always sufficient to understand the full informational content of that record. It is often helpful, and sometimes necessary, to be familiar with the cultural context in which the record was created. Here are three examples.

Interpreting Italian Terms. Because of numerous and distinct dialects, a word may take on different meanings in different parts of Italy. In addition, a word might signify one thing in one century and something else in another. Records created in mountainous terrain may contain terms peculiar to occupations of that setting, such as viniculture or mining, while records created in coastal towns may contain words peculiar to seafaring activities. Even a term as deceptively simple as *fattoria* or *podere*, translated in Italian-English dictionaries as "farm," can mislead American researchers who do not know what constitutes a farm in Italy.

You might picture farms as they exist in New England or the Midwest, with neighboring families separated by miles of cultivated fields or open pasture. In Italy, farmers reside together in the village, along with neighbors of all other trades and professions. Their adjoining houses line the narrow streets, creating the quaint environment that tourists from around the world visit Italy to experience. The farmers' fields and pastures surround the village. Up to the twentieth century, small livestock were kept at home, in the courtyard or ground level of the farmer's house. Large herds and flocks remained on the farmer's land beyond the town limits.

In short, a farm in Italy is different from a farm in the United States. You have to know the cultural context of a word to understand what it meant to your ancestors—and to get your ancestral stories straight!

Italian Cemeteries. Italian cemeteries are different too. Do not picture rolling grassy expanses with leafy trees and headstones marking individual graves. In Italy, burials are above ground, in mausoleums. Cemeteries are cities of the dead, with narrow streets and block after block of marble mausoleums, like apartment buildings. Some are low-rise, just one or two levels. But many are six or even eight feet high, containing tiers of graves, maybe four or five on top of one another like deep drawers, each about three feet wide and two feet high.

As you navigate the canyons of these necropolises, the "faithful departed" stare out at you. Rows and rows of faces watch you pass, for it is customary to adorn each grave with a portrait photograph of the deceased.

Some wealthy Italian families own their own mausoleums. As family members die, old caskets are removed to make room for new ones. The bones from the removed caskets are dropped into the ossuary beneath the mausoleum. As successive burials occur, a marble plaque on the exterior of the mausoleum is inscribed with the names and death dates of the family members who have been buried inside—a rich resource indeed for the lucky family historian.

The vast majority of Italian families, however, do not own their own mausoleums. Deceased members are laid in graves that are leased, generally for a period of twenty or thirty years. At the end of that time, if a surviving family member does not renew the lease, the casket is pulled out of the mausoleum like a drawer and the bones are placed in the common ossuary serving the entire cemetery. This practice has doomed to perpetual anonymity the Italian *popolino*, as no marble plaque remains to bear witness to their names and dates of death.

Therefore, unless your family was titled or just plain rich, you should not expect to discover and gaze upon the graves of your pre-twentieth-century forebears. Those graves will have changed occupants many times over the years!

***Detto* (Called).** You may be astounded to discover that some of your Italian ancestors were known by two surnames. Some old *stato civile* and *atti notarili* identify interested parties by both a hereditary surname and a *detto*, a second designation by which they were known within the community. A *detto* is more than an individual's nickname, because it not only appears in written records (where nicknames are very rarely found), but was used by multiple members of the family, often for more than one generation.

For example, the 1891 document shown on page 174 records the death of "Iannizzi Salvatore Zanella" in the *comune* of Mammola, *provincia* of Reggio-Calabria—the very toe of the Italian boot. As was customary (discussed under "Certificato di Stato di Famiglia"), the surname, Iannizzi,

Death record, 1891, of Salvatore Iannizzi. His name appears on the eleventh and twelfth lines of the document as "Iannizzi Salvatore Zanella." It was customary to put the surname before the given name. Note also the use of the additional name, Zanella, a *detto* by which this family was known for several generations. (*Photocopied document courtesy of Marcia Iannizzi Melnyk.*)

precedes the given name, Salvatore. But notice the additional name, Zanella, that follows. Though the word *detto* does not appear in this instance (sometimes it does and sometimes it does not), Zanella was indeed a *detto* used by this family for several generations.

How can we be sure of this? 1) Salvatore Iannizzi and his relatives always appear in the records of Mammola with their surnames, but only in *some* instances, not all, is the *detto* appended. 2) The *detto* does not appear on their *atti di nascita*, but it does appear on a variety of subsequent records. 3) Individuals bearing the *detto* Zanella, regardless of what their surnames were—Iannizzi as well as others—all fit into the same family tree. 4) The *detto* appears only in the records of Mammola. Individuals born in neighboring towns do not appear in the records with the *detto* until they move to Mammola and marry into this clan. Only then do records show the *detto* annexed to their names. 5) Zanella does not appear in any of the records of Mammola as a surname.

The custom of using a *detto* appears to have been much more prevalent in some *comuni* than others. In some places the practice was not observed at all. This is just another reflection of the wide variation you will find in records created throughout the Italian peninsula and islands over the course of centuries.

In short, for you to reap the greatest harvest from your examination of Italian records, you should familiarize yourself with the history of the people, the place and the time when those records were created. You do this by seeking out and reading books about the *comune, provincia* or *regione* where your ancestors lived, as recommended in Chapter 2 under "Italian Local History."

But there is another way to learn about the customs, traditions and dialect of your ancestors: familiarize yourself as much as possible with the *un*written history of their *paese*—that is, with its *oral* history.

Local Oral Lore

When you begin to correspond with relatives in Italy or with archivists, librarians or a hired professional genealogist, or when you visit your ancestral town in person, be sure to inquire about local oral history. Every corner of Italy is rich in lore that is passed on orally from generation to generation, and only the residents of that particular *paese* can relate it from memory.

You will not find it in books, because it is not written down. Or if someone *has* committed it to writing, you will discover it probably as a fascicle of typescript or manuscript pages lying in a parish archives or local library. Often it was the pastor of a rural parish, the *parroco* (a man of some education and an intellectual penchant with no other way to exercise it), who took an interest in the history of his community. He may have simply organized the parish archives and mined those old registers for his material. Or he may have examined other local records as well, and then assembled the information into a historical narrative.

One example is *Il Prezioso* (*The Precious Book*) found in the *biblioteca comunale* of Erice, a town near Trapani, Sicily. In the late seventeenth century the town's *parroco*, Don Vito Carvini, penned this manuscript in Latin on a thousand folios of vellum (lambskin). *Il Prezioso* tells part of the story of the *comune* of Erice as derived from original sixteenth- and seventeenth-century notarial and parish records, some of which have since disappeared. It contains a wealth of genealogical information about some of Erice's early families. For instance, six generations of the Giannitrapani family can be established by combining the information from several entries in the text of *Il Prezioso*.

In the villages of your ancestors, therefore, await sources you could never have known existed, could never have found outside the *comune*. Always bear in mind, though, that oral traditions are by their very nature unreliable in every detail. The stories are altered slightly, simplified or embellished with every retelling. It is best to verify their content against the community's original records.

Plan Your Transportation and Lodging

Plan your transportation and lodging as thoroughly as possible before crossing the Atlantic. Most places in Italy are easily accessible by rail or bus, but for some, you must rent a car. Learning the transportation situation in the region where your ancestors lived will save you a great deal of time and aggravation.

Also, not every *comune* has a hotel or *pensione* (small hotel where breakfast is included in the price of a night's stay). Italian government tourist offices in major U.S. cities, such as New York, Chicago and San Francisco, can often furnish more detailed and pertinent information for your trip than can U.S. travel agents. Italian tourist offices usually have the names and addresses of all categories of lodgings from four or five stars down to *pensioni* listed by province or region. (The government sets the price for each category.) They can also supply transportation and restaurant information for the cities you expect to visit (not the small towns), as well as superb road maps.

But the most expedient and convenient source of travel information is probably the Internet. Here are just two of the many informative and helpful sites:

Windows on Italy (**http://library.trinity.wa.edu.au/subjects/languages/italian/italy.htm**). This site contains information provided by the *Istituto Geografico De Agostini* regarding Italy today: historical sketches, administration, geography, population, economy, tourism and maps of every region, and information about major *comuni*, all in English.

Istituto Geografico De Agostini (**www.deagostini.it**). This website is a veritable newsmagazine in Italian, containing essays on the history, art, culture, and current events of Italy. The site is *not* genealogical, but provides helpful background information.

In Italy Online (**www.initaly.com**). Owned and operated by Words in Pictures, this site resembles a travel guide for Americans, offering travel tips; practical information about accommodations in Italy, weather, customs, transportation and what to do and see in each region; and related products for sale, such as maps and guidebooks.

A letter to the *sindaco* in the *municipio* can also clarify these matters . . . and prepare the way to your ancestral *paese*.

Closing

Italians do not have to search to learn who their grandparents were, or where they lived, or how they lived, or who their great-grandparents were either. They already know. Every day they live their heritage. For Italians have tended, until recent times, to remain for generations in the *comune* of their birth—the *comune* of their ancestors. This is due to the profound love of *famiglia* and the strong attachment to *paese* for which Italians are justly famed.

In the United States, however, Americans of Italian descent, cut off two or three generations ago from their families' roots, must engage in research to rediscover those roots. Understandably, Italian Americans in ever increasing numbers are taking up genealogy. The endeavor requires learning new information and mastering new skills; it calls for determination and patience too. Hopefully, this manual will help make your quest for your personal heritage a pleasant and enlightening journey. Its explanation of the genealogical process, its descriptions of historical resources at home and abroad, and its many suggestions and caveats should assist you in reaching back to your own family's *comune natale* (native town).

Once you have discovered that *comune natale*, it is often possible to trace your ancestors back two, three or more centuries, perhaps even to the late Middle Ages, so tenaciously did generation upon generation cling to one another and to their native soil. It is precisely that profound

179

love of *famiglia*, that strong attachment to *paese*, that makes their voyage to America all the more wondrous, all the more poignant.

The break was a traumatic one. The rift was decisive and permanent. It marked the last chapter of your Italian family history. It marked the first chapter in your American family history. It is a saga worth exploring and retelling, for it is your own.

The more you learn about who your ancestors were, the more you learn about who you are—and the more you appreciate what it means to be an Italian American.

Buona fortuna!

Bibliographic Note

This manual contains numerous statements of fact, yet cites no sources for them. Here is the explanation. In 1993, when *Finding Italian Roots* first appeared, documentation was not considered an essential component of genealogy manuals. The information this book contained was drawn from the author's experience researching his own Italian roots, as well as from his years of reading and teaching in the subject area. Such was the accepted standard of the day.

Today, however, the importance of documentation is being stressed in the field of genealogy. Besides conferring credibility on the genealogical work, proper documentation allows users to consult the sources the author consulted. Nevertheless, at this advanced stage in its life, to go back and provide a source note for every statement of fact in *Finding Italian Roots* would be a tedious task of dubious value. Readers interested in delving more deeply into any aspect of Italian genealogical research are encouraged to use the enlarged and updated **Select Bibliography** to do so.

To help readers access key works that address their particular interests, the Select Bibliography is broken down into thirteen topic categories. Most of the works cited contain notes and a bibliography, or at least an informative preface or introduction, for readers who wish to pursue a more scholarly investigation of the topic.

The corpus of published literature about Italian immigration and the Italian-American experience is colossal and continually growing, hence the use of the term "select." Nevertheless, it is hoped that the Select Bibliography constitutes an adequate entrée into the vast realm of research discussed in *Finding Italian Roots* and compensates for the manual's lack of documentation.

GLOSSARY

H ere is a list of all the Italian words used in this
guide, as well as a selection of other Italian nouns
that an American is likely to encounter when searching Italian records. It is intended as a springboard to further investigation of the Italian language. For more extensive glossaries, see the "Genealogical Word List—Italian" at
www.familysearch.org, as well as "Italian Occupations—
English Translations" in *POINTers*, vol. 16, no. 2 (summer
2002): 16–18. (Plurals are given in parentheses.)

Famiglia (Famiglie) = **Family**

antenato (antenati) = ancestor
albero genealogico (alberi genealogici) = family tree
bambina (bambine) = child (feminine)
bambino (bambini) = child (masculine)
bimba (bimbe) = baby (fem.)
bimbo (bimbi) = baby (masc.)
bisnonna (bisnonne) = great-grandmother
bisnonno (bisnonni) = great-grandfather
capostipite = founder of the family; earliest ancestor
cavaliere = knight; sir
cognome (cognomi) = surname
cugina (cugine) = cousin (fem.)
cugino (cugini) = cousin (masc.)
detto = called; also known as
don = title of respect for a man

donna = title of respect for a woman
famiglia nobile (famiglie nobili) = noble family
famiglia notabile (famiglie notabili) = noteworthy family
famiglia estinte (famiglie estinti) = extinct family
famiglia fiorente (famiglie fiorenti) = flourishing family
fanciulla (fanciulle) = baby girl
fanciullo (fanciulli) = baby boy
femmina (femmine) = female
fratello (fratelli) = brother
genealogia = genealogy
genitore (genitori) = parent; father
genitrice (genitrici) = mother
genitori ignoti = parents unknown
madre (madre) = mother
madre ignota = mother unknown
maestro (maestri) = master craftsman; teacher
mafioso (mafiosi) = member of the Mafia
maschio (or) *maschile* = male
nobilità = nobility
nobiliario (nobiliari) = book of nobility
nome (nomi) = name
nonna (nonne) = grandmother
nonno (nonni) = grandfather
padre (padri) = father
padre ignoto = father unknown
padre incerto = father uncertain
padrina (padrine) = godmother
padrino (padrini) = godfather
parente (parenti) = relative
persona (persone) = person
sorella (sorelle) = sister
zia (zie) = aunt
zio (zii) = uncle

Stato (Stati) = State

campagna = countryside
campagnuolo (*campagnuoli*) = countryman
capo luogo (*capi luoghi*) = provincial capital
carta d'identità = identification card
casa (*case*) = house
casa comunale (*case comunali*) = town hall
città (*citte*) = city
cittadina (*cittadine*) = citizen (fem.)
cittadino (*cittadini*) = citizen (masc.)
classe di leva (*classi di leva*) = conscription class, group
comune (*comuni*) = town
contadina (*contadine*) = peasant woman
contadino (*contadini*) = peasant man
distretto (*distretti*) = district
distretto militare (*distretti militari*) = military district
distretto notarile (*distretti notarili*) = notarial district
frazione (*frazioni*) = village; hamlet
gotico notarile = notarial gothic script
Italia = Italy
italianità = Italian-ness; state of being Italian
italiana (*italiane*) = Italian (fem.)
italiano (*italiani*) = Italian (masc.); the Italian language
leva = conscription; draft
ministero (*ministeri*) = ministry
municipio (*municipi*) = town hall
paesana (*paesane*) = countrywoman
paesano (*paesani*) = countryman
paese (*paesi*) = countryside; neighborhood
patria (*patrie*) = fatherland
polizia = police
popolazione (*popolazioni*) = population
popolino = common people; the masses
popolo = people

prefettura (prefetture) = prefect
provincia (provincie) = province
questura (questure) = police station
re (re) = king
regione (regioni) = region
regno (regni) = kingdom
sindaco (sindachi) = mayor
ufficio (uffici) = office
ufficiale (ufficiali) = officer

Archivio (Archivi) = Archives

allegato (allegati) = annexed document
annotazione (annotazioni) = annotation
annuario (annuari) = annual; yearbook
araldica = heraldry
archivio centralo dello stato = national archives
archivio comunale (archivi comunali) = town archives
archivio di stato (archivi di stato) = state archives
archivio ecclesiastico (archivi ecclesiastichi) = ecclesiastical
    archives
archivio genealogico (archivi genealogichi) = genealogical
    archives
archivio municipale (archivi municipali) = town archives
Archivio Segreto del Vaticano = Secret Archives of the
    Vatican
atto (atti) = record; deed
atto di nascita (atti di nascita) = birth record
*atto della solenna promessa di celebrare il matrimonio
    (atti della solenna promessa di celebrare il matrimonio)* =
    marriage record
atto di decesso (atti di decesso) = death record
atto di morto (atti di morto) = death record
bastardelli notarili = index of notarial records
beni immobili = real estate

beni mobili = personal estate
bibliografia (bibliografie) = bibliography
biblioteca (biblioteche) = library
biblioteca comunale (biblioteche comunali) = town library
biblioteca nazionale (biblioteche nazionali) = national library
biblioteca pubblica statale (biblioteche pubbliche statali) =
    public state library
biografia (biografie) = biography
blasone (blasoni) = coat of arms
carta (carte) = map
carta topografica (carte topografiche) = topographical map
catalogo (cataloghi) = catalogue
catasto (catasti) = tax assessment; tax list
censimento (censimenti) = census
censo (censi) = census
certificato (certificati) = certificate
certificato anagrafico (certificati anagrafici) = certificate of
    birth, marriage or death
certificato di residenza (certificati di residenza) = certificate of
    residency
certificato di stato di famiglia (certificati di stato di famiglia) =
    certificate of family status
*certificato di situazione di famiglia (certificati di situazione di
    famiglia)* = certificate of family status
cimitero (cimiteri) = cemetery
direttore (direttori) = director
dizionario (dizionari) = dictionary
documento (documenti) = document
emigrazione = emigration
enciclopedia (enciclopedie) = encyclopedia
fu = deceased (masc.)
fue = deceased (fem.)
genealogia (genealogie) = genealogy
giornale (giornali) = newspaper
guida (guide) = guide

immobiliare = real estate
indice decennale (*indici decennali*) = ten-year cumulative
    index
istituto (*istituti*) = institute
libro (*libri*) = book
minuta (*minute*) = rough draft
mobiliare = furniture
morto (*morti*) = dead person
nascita (*nascite*) = birth
notaio (*notai*) = notary
passaporto (*passaporti*) = passport
proietto (*proietti*) = foundling
projetto (*projetti*) = foundling
promessa (*promesse*) = promise
registro (*registri*) = register
registro degli uffici di leva (*registri degli uffici di leva*) =
    register of the office of conscription
registro dell'emigrazione e passaporti (*registri dell'emigrazione
    e passaporti*) = register of emigration and passports
registro delle unversità (*registri delle unversità*) = university
    register
registro di popolazione (*registri di popolazione*) = population
    register
residenza (*residenze*) = residence
ricerca (*ricerche*) = research
riveli = tax declarations
sezione (*sezioni*) = department; branch
stato civile = vital records
stemma (*stemme*) = coat of arms
storia (*storie*) = history
ufficiale di anagrafe (*ufficiali di anagrafe*) = census official
ufficiale di stato civile (*ufficiali di stato civile*) = official of
    vital records
ufficio anagrafico (*uffici anagrafici*) = office of the census
ufficio di anagrafe (*uffici di anagrafe*) = office of the census

ufficio di stato civile (uffici di stato civile) = office of vital records

Chiesa (Chiese) = Church

amica (amiche) = friend (fem.)
amico (amici) = friend (mas.)
anima (anime) = soul
archivio parrocchiale (archivi parrocchiali) = parish archives
archivio diocesano (archivi diocesani) = diocesan archives
archivio vescovile (archivi vescovili) = bishop's archives
arciprete (arcipreti) = head priest
atto di battesimo (atti di battesimo) = baptismal record
atto di matrimonio (atti di matrimonio) = marriage record
atto di sepoltura (atti di sepoltura) = burial record
atto di seppellimento (atti di seppellimento) = burial record
atto integrale (atti integrali) = complete record
battesimo (battesimi) = baptism
besogno (besogni) = need
cara = dear (fem.)
caro = dear (masc.)
Chiesa Cattolica = Catholic Church
Chiesa Madre = Mother Church
Chiesa Madrice = Mother Church
cresima (cresime) = confirmation
decessa (decesse) = deceased person (fem.)
decesso (decessi) = deceased person (masc.)
defunta (defunte) = deceased person (fem.)
defunto (defunti) = deceased person (masc.)
diocesi (diocesi) = diocese
Duomo = Mother Church
legati = legacies
matrimonio (matrimoni) = marriage
parrocchia (parrocchie) = parish
parroco (parrochi) = pastor

prete (preti) = priest
Protestanto (Protestanti) = Protestant
registro parrocchiale (registri parrocchiali) = parish registers
sacerdote (sacerdoti) = priest
sepoltura (sepolture) = burial
seppellimento (seppellimenti) = burial
stato delle anime = parish census
Valdesi = Waldenses; Waldensians
vescovo (vescovi) = bishop

Sinagoga (Sinagoghe) = Synagogue

ebrea (ebrei) = Jew (fem.)
ebreo (ebrei) = Jew (masc.)
ghetto (ghetti) = Jewish quarter
giudaico = Jewish

Miscellaneous Words Used in the Text

bottaio (bottai) = cooper (maker of wooden casks, barrels, tubs)
bracciale (bracciali) = laborer
bracciante (braccianti) = farmhand
buona fortuna = good luck
caffettiere (caffettieri) = cafe owner, operator
Casse di Risparmio Postale = Postal Savings Bank
cecità = blindness
fattoria (fattorie) = farm
grazie = thanks
grazie tante = many thanks
inglese = English; the English language
latifondo (latifondi) = large estate
mariolo (marioli) = Jew's harp; rogue
Mezzogiorno = southern Italy and Sicily (literally, "Noon")
Ministero dell'Interno = Ministry of the Interior

molto grazie = thanks very much
no = no
nobilità = nobility
oro = gold
pensione (pensioni) = small hotel; boarding house
piazza (piazze) = town square
podere (poderi) = farm; plot of land
sette = seven
si = yes
società = society or guild
stessa = same (fem.)
stesso = same (masc.)
storia = history
tenuta (tenute) = estate
trafficante (trafficanti) = merchant

BIBLIOGRAPHY

H ere is a list of all the published works, Internet websites and Italian genealogical societies cited in this guide, as well as a selection of other works representative of the broad spectrum of published resources available to assist Americans tracing Italian ancestry.

Manuals and Guides

Carmack, Sharon DeBartolo. *Italian-American Family History: A Guide to Researching and Writing About Your Heritage*. Baltimore: Genealogical Publishing Co., 1997.
How to discover and write the story of your immigrant ancestors' experience in the United States.

Cole, Trafford R. *Italian Genealogical Records: How to Use Italian Civil, Ecclesiastical & Other Records in Family History Research*. Salt Lake City: Ancestry, 1995.
Guide to advanced research in Italian records. Contains sample letters for obtaining records from repositories in Italy.

Colletta, John Philip. *They Came in Ships: A Guide to Finding Your Immigrant Ancestor's Arrival Record*, 3rd ed. Orem, Utah: Ancestry, 2002.
A comprehensive manual, with extensive bibliography, for finding your immigrant ancestors' ships, colonial times to twentieth century.

Guelfi Camajani, Guelfo. *Genealogy in Italy*. Firenze: Istituto Genealogico Italiano, 1979.
Brief general overview in English of Italian archival resources.

Guelfi Camajani, Luigi. *Alcuni Appunti sulle Ricerche Genealogiche in Italia*. Stockholm: Bureau du Vème Congrès International des Sciences Généalogique et Héraldique, 1960.
Brief and general, but does illustrate how much parish archives differ from one parish to another throughout Italy.

Nelson, Lynn. *A Genealogist's Guide to Discovering Your Italian Ancestors.* Cincinnati: Betterway Books, 1997.

The Internet

There are *hundreds* of websites useful for Italian genealogy. Here is a sampling:

Allen County Public Library (**www.acpl.lib.in.us**). One of the country's premier genealogical collections.

American Family Immigration History Center (**www.ellisislandrecords.org**). Digitized images of the passenger arrival records of New York, 1892–1924, and a search engine for finding one passenger among the estimated twenty-two million names.

Ancestry.com (**www.ancestry.com**). Genealogical information and hundreds of databases, one of which is the *free* Social Security Death Index.

Archives of Italy (**www.archivi.beniculturali.it**). Guide to all of Italy's ninety-five *archivi di stato*, including descriptions of their collections and practical information for using them. In Italian.

Centro di Documentazione Ebraica Contemporanea (**www.cdec.it**). Huge collection of studies of Italy's Jewish communities and many specific families.

Centro di Studi sull'Ebraismo Italiano (**www.italcham.org.il/museum/italindex.html**). Large collection of books on Italian Jewry.

Circolo Calabrese (**www.circolocalabrese.org**). Help for researching Calabrian ancestors.

Cyndi's List (**www.cyndislist.com**). Links to numerous sites pertaining to Italian genealogy.

Family History Library (**www.familysearch.org**). Click on "Search," then "Research Helps," then "Italy," for much useful information, including sample letters in Italian, a glossary of Italian words and a research outline for Italian genealogy.

Immigration History Research Center (**www.umn.edu/ihrc**). Substantial collection of materials on the history of Italians in America, including the entire archives of the Order of the Sons of Italy in America.

In Italy Online (**www.initaly.com**). Guide for Americans traveling in Italy, including accommodations, weather, customs, transportation. Sells maps and guidebooks.

Institute for Diaspora Research (**www.tau.ac.il/humanities/institutes-index.html#diaspora**). Information and published works about the Jewish communities of Italy.

International Currency Express (**www.foreignmoney.com**). Commercial firm that provides checks in any currency.

Istituto Genealogico Italiano (**www.genealogia.it**). This private organization is the largest genealogical institution in Italy, and is compiling a general index to Italian genealogy, with up to four million surnames.

Istituto Geografico De Agostini (**www.deagostini.it**). Essays in Italian on the history, art, culture and current events of Italy.

Italian Ancestry (**www.ItalianAncestry.com**). Links to numerous sites containing useful information about Italian genealogy.

Italian Genealogical & Heraldic Institute (**www.regalis.com/institute.htm**). Private website of two professional genealogists who specialize in research for American clients.

Italian Genealogy Homepage (**http://italiangenealogy.tardio.com/html**). Essays in English about using the records of Italy. Sample letters.

Jewishgen (**www.jewishgen.org**). Excellent starting point for tracing Italian ancestors who were Jewish. Numerous links.

Libraries of Italy (**www.librari.beniculturali.it**). Spectacular site containing maps and information about all of Italy's state libraries.

Library of Congress (**www.loc.gov**). Searchable catalog of one of the largest genealogical collections in the U.S.

National Archives (**www.archives.gov**). Entrée into the mammoth body of historical federal records useful for American genealogy, including censuses, naturalizations, passenger arrival records, military service, passport applications, etc.

New York Public Library (**www.nypl.org**). Searchable catalog for the Library's huge genealogy department is at this site.

Sicilia in Dettaglio (**http://sicilia.indettaglio.it/ita/index.html**). Information about the 390 *comuni* of Sicily.

The Universal Currency Converter (**www.xe.com/ucc**). Converts dollars into euros and vice-versa.

U.S. Newspaper Program (**www.neh.gov/projects/usnp.html**). Clearinghouse for information about U.S. newspapers available nationwide.

Virgilio (**www.virgilio.it**). Italian telephone directories.

Vital Records (**www.cdc.gov/nchs/howto/w2w/w2welcom.htm**). Where to write for state records of birth, marriage, divorce and death.

Windows on Italy (**http://library.trinity.wa.edu.au/subjects/languages/italian/italy.htm**). Italy today: historical sketches, administration, geography, population, economy, tourism, map of every region and information about major *comuni*, all in English.

Research Aids

Andreozzi, John. *Guide to the Records of the Order of the Sons of Italy in America*. St. Paul, Minn.: Immigration History Research Center, 1988.
    Describes the Order's archives, now part of the substantial Italian-American collection in the Immigration History Research Center.

Archivio di Stato di Palermo: Inventario Sommario. Roma: Ministero dell'Interno, 1950.
    Catalog of major categories of holdings in the *archivio di stato* in Palermo.

Battelli, Giulio. *Lezioni di Paleografia*. Città del Vaticano, 1949.

Cappelli, Adriano. *Dizionario di Abbreviature Latine ed Italiane*, 6th ed. Milano: Editore Ulrico Hoepli, 1979.
    Dictionary of Latin and Italian abbreviations used in old Italian records.

Carmack, Sharon DeBartolo. "Using Social Security Records to Test an Italian-American Family Tradition." *National Genealogical Society Quarterly*, vol. 77, no. 4 (December 1989): 257–9.
    Demonstrates how Social Security records may be obtained and used to solve a genealogical problem.

_____. "The Genealogical Use of Social History: An Italian-American Example." *National Genealogical Society Quarterly*, vol. 79, no. 4 (December 1991): 284–8.
    Illustrates the importance of learning local history to understand ancestors' lives and motivations.

Cole, Trafford. "Regional References in Italian Genealogical Record Sources." *POINTers*, vol. 5, nos. 3 and 4 (Autumn and Winter 1991), and vol. 6, nos. 1 and 2 (Spring and Summer 1992).
    Series of four articles discussing regional differences among Italian records.

Colletta, John Philip. "The Italian Mayflowers." *Attenzione* (February 1984): 30–33.
    How to search the ships' passenger lists at the National Archives for immigrant ancestors from Italy.

_____. "Search and Discovery in Italy." *Attenzione* (March 1984): 34–37.
    How to prepare for a research trip to the Italian village of one's ancestors.

Eichholz, Alice, ed. *Ancestry's Redbook: American State, County and Town Sources*, rev. ed. Salt Lake City: Ancestry, Inc., 1992.
    Helpful in locating naturalization records made in county and municipal courts.

Everton Publishers. *Everton's Handybook,* 7th ed. Bountiful, Utah: Everton Publishers, 2000.
Another work useful in locating naturalization records.

Glazier, Ira A., and P. William Filby, eds. *Italians to America: Lists of Passengers Arriving at U.S. Ports.* Wilmington, Del.: Scholarly Resources, Inc., 1992–present. 16 vols. On-going.
So far, all passengers are New York arrivals; other ports will follow.

Guida delle Regioni d'Italia. 3 vols. Roma: Società Italiana per lo Studio dei Problemi Regionali, 1994/5. (published annually)
This superb directory of Italy lists, region-by-region, province-by-province, all *archivi di stato, biblioteche* and other political, cultural and touristic information.

Guida Generale degli Archivi di Stato Italiani. 4 vols. Roma: Ministero per i Beni Culturali e Ambientali, Ufficio Centrale per i Beni Archivistici, 1986.
Describes contents of all of Italy's *archivi di stato.*

Guida Monaci: Annuario Generale Italiano, 117th ed. Roma: Guide Monaci, 1991. (revised annually)
Practical guide to all of the governmental offices and agencies of Italy, including their addresses, names of directors, telephone numbers, etc.

Guide to Genealogical Research in the National Archives, 3rd ed. Washington, D.C.: National Archives Trust Fund Board, 2000.
Each chapter describes a different type of federal record of value to genealogists, including censuses, passenger arrivals, naturalizations, military service, etc.

Itinerari Archivistici Italiani. 20 pamphlets. Roma: Ministero per i Beni Culturali e Ambientali, Ufficio Centrale per i Beni Archivistici, n.d.
Superbly written and illustrated little volumes that present a brief overview of the documentary materials in the *archivi di stato* throughout Italy, plus practical information about their locations, hours of operation, photocopying services, etc.

Lewanski, Rudolf J., comp. *The Guide to Italian Libraries and Archives.* New York: Council for European Studies, 1979.
Describes Italian system of libraries and archives and gives a statistical profile of the major institutions.

Library of Congress. *Newspapers in Microform: United States, 1948–1983,* 2 vols. Washington, D.C.: Library of Congress, 1984.
Helps locate Italian language newspapers on microfilm.

Marraro, Francesco. *Repertorio delle Biblioteche Italiane.* Roma: Editoriale Cassia, 1989.

Lists by region, and thereunder by province, every library of Italy, with address, phone number, director's name and number of volumes.

Moody, Suzanna, and Joel Wurl, comps. and eds. *The Immigration History Research Center: A Guide to Collections.* New York: Greenwood Press, 1991.
Describes the Italian-American collection, approximately 1,400 items, including a microfilm copy of many Italian-American newspapers and the archives of the Order of the Sons of Italy in America.

Riippa, Timo, comp. *Report on the Italian American Newspaper Microfilming Project.* St. Paul, Minn.: Immigration History Research Center, University of Minnesota, 1992.
Catalog of Italian language newspapers microfilmed between 1985 and 1990, indicating the repository that holds the original.

Russo, Suzanne. "Lessons Learned in Italian Archives: What to Know Before You Go." *Association of Professional Genealogists Quarterly,* vol. xvii, no. 2 (June 2002): 61–65.

Schaefer, Christina K. *Guide to Naturalization Records of the United States.* Baltimore: Genealogical Publishing Co., 1997.
State-by-state description of naturalization records all over the country; not comprehensive, but helpful.

Stevens, Revalee. *North American Records in Italy: The Protestant Cemetery of Rome.* Baton Rouge, La.: Oracle Press, 1981.
Burial records of all Americans buried in Rome's Protestant cemetery.

_____. *Protestant Records in Italy: The Registers of St. Paul's Within-the-Walls.* Baton Rouge, La.: Oracle Press, 1985.
Baptismal, marriage and burial records of American citizens in the registers of Rome's largest Protestant Church.

Stych, F.S. *How to Find Out about Italy.* Oxford: Pergamon Press, 1970.
A guide to locating bibliographies and collections of works dealing with all aspects of Italian life and culture, including philosophy and religion, language and linguistics, social sciences, literature, genealogy and heraldry, and more.

Szucs, Loretto Dennis. *They Became Americans: Finding Naturalization Records and Ethnic Origins.* Salt Lake City: Ancestry, Inc., 1998.
Complete instruction; covers the topic thoroughly.

_____, and Sandra Hargreaves Luebking, eds. *The Source: A Guidebook of American Genealogy,* rev. ed. Salt Lake City: Ancestry, 1997.
Monumental guide to conducting genealogical research in every kind of U.S. source imaginable.

General Histories of Italians in America

Barolini, Helen, *et al. Images: A Pictorial History of Italian Americans,* 2nd ed. New York: Center for Migration Studies, 1986.
> Pictorial histories like this one are useful for background information.

Cordasco, Francesco. *Italian Americans: A Guide to Information Sources.* Detroit: Gale Research Co., 1978.
> Extensive bibliography of works on all aspects of the Italian experience in the United States.

Grossman, Ronald P. *The Italians in America.* Minneapolis: Lerner Publications, 1975.
> Historical overview mentioning a selection of famous Italian Americans.

LaGumina, Salvatore J. *An Album of the Italian American.* New York: Franklin Watts, 1972.
> General history, but some families and individuals are named.

LoGatto, Anthony F. *The Italians in America, 1492–1972.* Dobbs Ferry, N.Y.: Oceana Publications, 1973.
> A chronological outline.

Mangione, Jerre, and Ben Morreale. *La Storia: Five Centuries of the Italian American Experience.* New York: Perennial Books, 1992.

Rolle, Andrew F. *The Immigrant Upraised: Italian Adventurers and Colonists in an Expanding America.* Norman: University of Oklahoma Press, 1968.
> Notable for its chapter on Italians in Colorado and other mining communities.

Scarpaci, Vincenza. *A Portrait of the Italians in America.* New York: Scribner's Sons, 1983.
> Another pictorial history of merit.

Schiavo, Giovanni Ermenegildo. *The Italians in America before the Civil War.* New York: Vigo Press (for the Italian Historical Society), 1934.
> Traces the Italian presence in America from 1492 to the Civil War. Handy chronology and extensive bibliography, but no index.

_____. *The Italians in America before the Revolutionary War.* New York: Vigo Press, 1976.

Histories of Italian Communities in the United States

Fede, Frank Joseph. *Italians in the Deep South: Their Impact on Birmingham and the American Heritage.* Birmingham, Ala.: Black Belt Press, 1994.

Fiore, Alphonse T. *History of Italian Immigration in Nebraska.* [Omaha Public Library]

Guida degli Italiani del Copper County. Iron Mountain, Mich.: Ralph W. Secord Press, 1987. (Originally published in 1910.)

> Directory of Italians living in Copper County in 1810, including biographies of notable *"Pionieri della Colonia."*

Gumina, Deanna Paoli. *The Italians of San Francisco (1850–1930).* New York: Center for Migration Studies, 1977.

Juliani, Richard N. *Building Little Italy: Philadelphia's Italians Before Mass Migration.* Philadelphia: Penn State Press, 1998.

Mormino, Gary Ross. *Immigrants on the Hill: Italian-Americans in St. Louis, 1882–1982.* Urbana and Chicago: University of Illinois Press, 1986.

> History of the Italian community of St. Louis, naming many individuals and families.

_____, and George E. Pozzetta. *The Immigrant World of Ybor City: Italians and Their Latin Neighbors in Tampa, 1885–1985.* Urbana and Chicago: University of Illinois Press, 1987.

Riccio, Anthony V. *Portrait of an Italian-American Neighborhood: The North End of Boston.* New York: Center for Migration Studies, 1998.

Sandler, Gilbert. *The Neighborhood: The Story of Baltimore's Little Italy.* Baltimore, Md.: Bodine, 1974.

Schiavo, Giovanni Ermenegildo. *The Italians in Chicago: A Study of Americanization.* Chicago: Italian American Publishing Co., 1928. Reprinted 1970.

> Much biographical and genealogical information about earliest Italians in and around Chicago.

Starr, Dennis J. *The Italians of New Jersey: A Historical Introduction and Bibliography.* Newark: New Jersey Historical Society, 1985.

> Bibliography of published works about Italians in New Jersey.

Weaver, Glenn. *The Italian Presence in Colonial Virginia.* New York: Center for Migration Studies, 1988.

> Thorough account of Italians who emigrated from England to colonial Virginia, naming individuals and families.

Yans-McLaughlin, Virginia. *Family and Community: Italian Immigrants in Buffalo, 1880–1930.* Ithaca, N.Y.: Cornell University Press, 1978.

Collective Biographies of Italian Americans

Carlevale, Joseph William. *Americans of Italian Descent in New Jersey.* Clifton, N.J.: North Jersey Press, 1950.

> Over 3,000 biographical sketches.

_____. *Leading Americans of Italian Descent in Massachusetts.* Plymouth, Mass.: Memorial Press, 1946.

> Four thousand biographical sketches.

_____. *Leading Americans of Italian Descent in Philadelphia and Vicinity.* Philadelphia: G.S. Ferguson, 1954.

_____. *Who's Who among Americans of Italian Descent in Connecticut.* New Haven: Carlevale Publishing Co., 1942.
> Fourteen hundred biographical sketches.

Caselli, U. Piola, ed. *Italo-American Business Directory.* New York: Caselli, 1904.
> Lists officers of the Italian Chamber of Commerce in the United States, the American Chamber of Commerce in Italy, and hundreds of American businessmen of Italian descent, as well as many Italian businessmen, along with their respective businesses.

Casso, Evans J. *Staying in Step: A Continuing Italian Renaissance (A Saga of American-Italians in Southeast United States).* New Orleans: Quadriga Press, 1984.
> Biographical information about hundreds of Italian Americans of Louisiana, Texas, Mississippi, Alabama, Georgia, South Carolina and North Carolina. Indexed.

Directory of Italian-Americans in Commerce and Professions. Chicago: Continental Press, 1937.
> State-by-state listing of Italian Americans in the business world in 1937.

Library of Congress. *Italians in the Northwest.* Exhibition catalog. Washington, D.C.: Library of Congress, 1992.

Dictionaries of Italian Surnames

Cole, Trafford R. "The Origin, Meaning and Changes in Major Italian Surnames." *The Genealogical Helper,* 36 (March–April 1982): 11–14.

DeFelice, Emidio. *Dizionario dei Cognomi Italiani.* Milan: Arnoldo Mondadori, 1978.
> Discusses the origins and literal meanings of Italian surnames in general; includes explanations of many specific family names.

Fucilla, Joseph G. *Our Italian Surnames.* Evanston, Ill.: Chandler's, 1949. [Reprint: Baltimore: Genealogical Publishing Company, 1996.]
> Origins and meanings of numerous Italian surnames.

Schaert, Samuele. *I Cognomi degli Ebrai d'Italia.* Firenze: Casa Editrice Israel, 1925.
> Surveys numerous Jewish family names of Italy.

Italian National Biography

Boschetti, Anton Ferrante, ed. *Catalogo delle Famiglie Celebri Italiane.* Modena: Società Tipografica Modenese, 1930.

Dizionario Biografico degli Italiani. Roma: Istituto della Enciclopedia Italiana, 1960–present. 56 volumes to date.
> When finished, this will be the most complete Italian national biography in print. "A" through "G" are done.

Dizionario dei Siciliani Illustri. Palermo: F. Ciumi, 1939.

Enciclopedia Biografica e Bibliografica Italiana. Roma: Istituto Editoriale Italiano, 1941.
> This multi-volume set includes several series, such as military, the arts, politics, etc. Substantial biographical and genealogical content.

Genealogies of Italian Families

Albo Nazionale: Famiglie Nobili dello Stato Italiano. [Roma?]: Associazione Historiae Fides, 1965.
> Listing of titled Italian families bearing arms.

Battilana, Natale, ed. *Genealogie delle Famiglie Nobili di Genova.* Genova: Fratelli Pagano, 1825.
> Alphabetical listing of noble families of Genoa. Similar works are available for all major cities of Italy.

Colaneri, Giustino. *Bibliografia Araldica e Genealogica d'Italia.* Roma: Ermanno Loescher & Co., 1904.
> Bibliography of works on Italian genealogy and heraldry in the *Biblioteca Casanatense* in Rome. Mostly rare histories of noble families published in the sixteenth, seventeenth, eighteenth and nineteenth centuries.

Di Casalgerardo, A. Mango. *Nobiliario di Sicilia.* Palermo: Libreria Internazionale A. Reber, 1912.
> Alphabetical listing of noble families of Sicily, with descriptions of their coats of arms. Similar works are available for all of Italy's regions.

Di Crollalanza, Giovanni B. *Dizionario Storico-Blasonico delle Famiglie Nobili e Notabili Italiane Estinti e Fiorenti.* 3 vols. Pisa: Presso la Direzione del Giornale Araldico, 1886–96.
> The "granddaddy" of Italian heraldry.

Gheno, Antonio. *Contributo alla Bibliografia Genealogica Italiana.* Bologna: Forni, 1924. [Reprint 1971.]
> Bibliography of published genealogies of Italian families— mostly ancient and illustrious and titled.

Gravina, V. Palizzolo. *Il Blasone in Sicilia.* Bologna: Forni, 1972. [Reprint of original Palermo edition of 1871–75.]

Guelfi Camajani, Luigi, ed. *Le Famiglie Nobili e Notabili Italiane.* Firenze: Archivio Storico Araldico Nobiliare, 1969.

Libro d'Oro della Nobilità Italiana. Roma: Collegio Araldico, 1989 (and later, updated every few years).
>Single-volume directory of living Italians who hold titles.

Mendola, Luigi. "A Guide to Italian Heraldry." *POINTers*, vol. 5, no. 4 (Winter 1991).

Pavoncello, Nello. *Antiche Famiglie Ebraiche Italiane.* Roma: Carucci Editore, 1982.
>First volume of a proposed series composed of articles reprinted from the 1957–1960 issues of the *Settimanale Israel.* Gives histories of twenty Jewish families.

Pisa, Franco. "Parnassim: Le Grande Famiglie Ebraiche Italiane dal Secolo XI al XIX." *Annuario di Studi Ebraici*, ed. by Ariel Toaff. Roma: Carucci Editore, 1980–84.
>Sketches of prominent Jewish families of Italy.

Scorza, Angelo M. G. *Enciclopedia Araldica Italiana.* Genova: Studio Ricerche Storiche, 1955.
>Coats of arms and genealogical tables.

Spreti, Vittorio, *et al. Enciclopedia Storico-Nobiliare Italiana.* 8 vols. Milano: Enciclopedia Storico-Nobiliare Italiana, 1928–35.
>Another work of heraldry covering the entire country of Italy.

Maps and Gazetteers of Italy

Allgemeines Geografisches Statistisches Lexikon aller Osterreichischen Staaten. 11 vols.
>Since a portion of northern Italy was part of the Austro-Hungarian Empire up to 1919, this gazetteer may be needed to locate and identify Italian towns in the Alps.

Annuario Cattolico d'Italia. Roma: Editoriale Italiana, 1978–79 (and later, published yearly).
>Lists by diocese all parishes of Italy.

Annuario delle Diocesi d'Italia. [Roma?]: Marietti Editori, Ltd., 1951.
>For every parish in Italy, gives name of parish, its diocese, *comune, provincia* and pastor (as of 1951). Regional maps show all dioceses and parishes.

Annuario Generale, Comuni e Frazioni d'Italia. Milano: Touring Club Italiano, 1968 and later (every 5 years).
>Lists all of Italy's *comuni* and *frazioni* in alphabetical order, with substantial information about each one.

Euro-Atlas: ITALY. Maspeth, N.Y.: American Map Corporation, 1998. (This is the U.S. edition of a series of atlases of European countries published in Germany.)
>Detailed maps of every corner of Italy, including street maps of major cities, with extensive gazetteer.

Grande Carta Topografica del Regno d'Italia. Firenze: Istituto Geografico
Militare, 1882–present (updated periodically). 277 maps.
   Most detailed atlas of Italy available.
Guida delle Regioni d'Italia. Roma: Società Italiana per lo Studio dei
Problemi Regionali, 1994/5. 3 vols. (published annual--ˋ
   Political, administrative, econ°m⁙˙
   twenty regions of Italy; inclᵤ
   and all *bibliotheche.*
Nuovo Dizionario dei Comuni e Frazion⸱
Dizionario Voghera dei Comuni, 1ᒑ
   Lists every *comune* and *frazio*
   tion.

Italian Local History

Bilello, Francesco. *I Sette Re di Agr*
Quartararo, 1975.
   Example of a history of a *provir*
Calimani, Riccardo. *Storia del Ghetto di ˌ*
1985.
   Excellent example of Jewish loc
   into English: Wolfthal, Katherine
   of Venice. New York: M. Evans a
   bibliography.
Carvini, Vito. *Il Prezioso.* A manuscript hiˌ   ᵤₘᵤₙₑ of Erice,
Province of Trapani, Sicily, penned in Latin in the late seventeenth
century.
Consonni, Manuela M., ed. *Bibliotheca Italo-Ebraica: Bibliografia per la
Storia degli Ebrai in Italia, 1986–1995.* Rome: Menorah, 1997.
   Continues Luzzatto's work cited below.
De Stefano, Antonino, ed. *Il Registro Notarile di Giovanni Maiorana, 1297–
1300.* Volume II of *Memorie e Documenti di Storia Siciliana, Documenti.*
Palermo: Presso l'Istituto di Storia Patria, 1943.
   Example of published notarial records.
Giannitrapani, Domenico. *Il Monte Erice, Oggi San Giuliano: Paesaggio,
Storia e Costumi.* Bologna: Zanichelli, 1892.
   Example of a history of a *comune.*
Luzzatto, Aldo. *Biblioteca Italo-Ebraica.* Milano: Franco Angeli Libri, 1989.
   Huge bibliography of works published 1974–85 on Jews in Italy.
   Indexed. Updated to 1995 by Consonni, cited above.
Musca, Giosue, ed. *Storia della Puglia,* 2 vols. Bari: Mario Adda Editore,
1979.
   Example of a history of a *regione.*

Russo, Rocco. *Casteldaccia nella Storia della Sicilia*. [Palermo?]: Edizioni Arti Grafiche "Battaglia," 1961.
　　Another example of a history of a *comune*.
Sacerdoti, Annie. *Guida all'Italia Ebraica*. Casale Monferrato: Casa Editrice Marietti, 1986.
　　Survey of all Jewish communities of Italy, past and present, with research information for each. English edition: DeLossa, Richard F., trans. *Guide to Jewish Italy*. Brooklyn: Israelowitz Publishing, 1989.
Simonsohn, Shlomo. *History of the Jews in the Duchy of Mantua*. Tel Aviv: Ktav Publishing House, Inc., 1977.
　　Volume 17 of the Publications of the Diaspora Research Institute. A superb example of Jewish local history.
_____. *The Jews of the Duchy of Milan*. 4 vols. Jerusalem: The Israel Academy of Sciences and Humanities, 1986.
　　Jewish records, Middle Ages to sixteenth century, in English translation with notes. Part of a proposed documentary history of the Jews of Italy.

Organizations and Their Publications

Italian Genealogical Group
Box 626
Bethpage, NY 11714-0626
www.italiangen.org/default.stm
Newsletter ten times a year

Italian Genealogical Society of America
P.O. Box 3572
Peabody, MA 01961-3572
www.Italianroots.org
Quarterly newsletter, *Lo Specchio*

POINT (Pursuing Our Italian Names Together)
P.O. Box 14966, Dept. PHP
Las Vegas, NE 89114-4966
http://point-pointers.net
Quarterly journal, *POINTers*

General Histories of Italy

Finley, M. I. *Ancient Sicily, To the Arab Conquest*. New York: Viking Press, 1968.

Smith, Denis Mack. *Italy: A Modern History*. Ann Arbor, Mich.: University of Michigan Press, 1969. [Revised and enlarged edition of original 1959 work.]

> Well-respected one-volume history of Italy. "Suggested Readings" section lists many more-detailed accounts of specific Italian periods, places and topics.

_____. *Medieval Sicily, 800–1713* and *Modern Sicily, After 1713*. 2 vols. New York: Viking Press, 1968.

> The definitive history of Sicily in English, written by a prominent scholar.